Demystifying Secondary Inclusion:
Powerful School-wide & Classroom Strategies

by Lisa Dieker, Ph.D.

DUDE PUBLISHING
A Division of
National Professional Resources, Inc.
Port Chester, New York

Library of Congress Cataloging-in-Publication Data

Dieker, Lisa.
Demystifying secondary inclusion : powerful
schoolwide and classroom strategies / by Lisa Dieker.
p. cm.
Includes bibliographical references and index.
ISBN 1-934032-02-6

1. Inclusive education. 2. Education, Secondary.
3. Youth with disabilities—Education (Secondary)
4. School management and organization. 5. Classroom
management.   I. Title.

LC1200.D54 2006   *371.9'046*
                    QBI06-600342

Acquisitions Editor: Helene M. Hanson
Associate Editor: Lisa L. Hanson
Production Editor, Cover Design: Andrea Cerone,
National Professional Resources, Inc., Port Chester, NY

© 2007 Lisa A. Dieker

Dude Publishing
A Division of National Professional Resources, Inc.
25 South Regent Street
Port Chester, New York 10573
Toll free: (800) 453-7461
Phone: (914) 937-8879

Visit our web site: www.NPRinc.com

Printed in the United States of America

ISBN 1-934032-02-6

To my husband, Rich, and our son, Joshua;

To children with disabilities who remind us what is truly important—
life, love, and laughter;

And, to all those who make a difference in the lives of these children.

Table of Contents

Acknowledgements

Special thanks for the support and inspiration of my husband and son who gave up several evenings with me so I could work on this book, which they know is so important in my heart. I would also like to thank all of the teachers in Rantoul, Illinois, who taught me so many foundational lessons about secondary schools and inclusion, and especially my dear friend and colleague, Janet Hill. To my professors and colleagues at Eastern Illinois University and University of Illinois, thank you for believing I might make a difference in the lives of children with disabilities. To my colleagues at the University of Wisconsin-Milwaukee and University of Central Florida, thanks for supporting me in following my dreams.

To my parents and my husband's parents, both of whom modeled so elegantly the lessons of inclusion by showing me the powerful outcomes that result when parents believe in children with disabilities and ensure that their children receive the greatest level of education possible to be wonderfully productive people in society.

A special thank you to Chris O'Brien and Christine Ogilvie, both of whom are dedicated teachers, respected doctoral students, and future leaders in the field: Chris, for his final edits and support with the production of the complementary video; and, Christine, who reviewed the chapters when I could no longer read another word. A warm and admiring thank you to Fran Vandiver and the amazing teachers and staff at PK Yonge School in Gainesville, FL, for so simply yet professionally sharing with me what they do everyday to make a difference in the lives of all students.

A very special thank you to the Hanson family: to Robert Hanson, for his faith in my work and message; to Angela, for her positive support; to Lisa, for her wonderful technical editing; and a heartfelt thank you to a kindred soul in special education and a new dear friend, Helene, who went above and beyond the job of an editor to make this work as meaningful as possible to the field of special education. Finally, to education students, teachers, teacher educators, administrators, parents and, most importantly, students who have taught me so many lessons about inclusive education and celebrating everyone.

Introduction

Never before has the field of secondary special education been confronted by such monumental challenges: High stakes testing, a more diverse student population, new requirements to ensure "highly qualified" teachers, just to name a few. Schools must focus on the needs of the students and families they serve while remaining aware of the competing challenges they face such as school budgets, teacher unions, pay raises, and classroom materials. Merely acknowledging the issues in these turbulent times is not sufficient. Instead, we must look for practical, meaningful solutions.

It has been my privilege to observe numerous middle and high schools throughout the country. In appreciation for the lessons I have learned from these visits, I want to share ideas, suggestions, and strategies that will help demystify the seemingly illusive goal of successful inclusive secondary education. These ideas are a reflection of the hard work of teachers and students who do not merely survive in inclusive secondary programs, but truly thrive, overcoming the ever-changing issues they face. These thriving schools and talented teachers never loose sight of their most important task, that of educating each and every child who enters the building.

I do not presume in life or in this book to have all the answers, but I believe that sharing experiences and observations of real teachers, schools, and classrooms can be beneficial in providing ideas for the creation of a more inclusive school and classroom environment. Whether you are enriching practices already in place, beginning a complete review of your school's current inclusive practices, or taking the first steps in the process, you will benefit from perusing the content and identifying those ideas that should or should not be considered as you work with a range of learners in your school and your classrooms.

The words "together we are better" are used as a mantra throughout this book. I have identified seven overarching and interdependent topics to provide a basic structure for inclusion: creating an inclusive school-wide culture, celebrating the success of all students, developing interdisciplinary collaboration, implementing effective co-teaching, establishing active learning environments, implementing successful instruction, and improving grading and student assessments.   By intent, these topics and their subtopics appear and reappear throughout the text, reinforcing their interactive relationship. The true measure of a school that successfully educates students with disabilities in the general education setting is the seamless interweaving of these seven topics into the fabric of the school culture and daily classroom activities, and the ability of all stakeholders vested in the education process to clearly understand and articulate this philosophy.

Chapters 1-3 of this book identify ways to ensure that students with disabilities are included in the general education environment of a school. Chapters 4-7 provide additional instructional strategies for embracing all learners and creating an inclusive classroom climate that facilitates effective learning outcomes. Chapter 8 presents concrete ways of preparing staff for the work required to develop and maintain an inclusive environment. Exhibits, charts, and extensive lists are provided throughout each chapter to illustrate successful practices of strong schools and classrooms. Additionally, each chapter ends with a set of questions to encourage reflection on current practice. Included at the end of this book is an extensive Resource section. The products included therein have been carefully selected to assist in the development, enrichment, and refinement of inclusive secondary practices.

While writing this book, I also had the pleasure of collaborating with National Professional Resources, Inc. on a video/DVD production entitled *7 Effective Strategies for Secondary Inclusion.* Encompassing the same content area as the video/DVD, this book enriches and expands upon its visual images and scenarios, providing additional ideas and examples from students and their outstanding teachers in successful, inclusive secondary schools. More details on *7 Effective Strategies for Secondary Inclusion* can be found on the back cover of this book or at www.NPRinc.com.

Schools that are successful in their inclusionary practices consistently focus on proven and promising practices for all students. Students are the center of planning and instruction, are engaged in the teaching-learning process, and develop self-advocacy skills. Students with disabilities are expected to leave school with both content knowledge and social skills that will ensure their future success. A sense of positive energy echoes in the hallways of an effective inclusive school; pictures of clubs and sports teams on the wall demonstrate a recognition of students and the strengths they bring to school; students smile and laugh as they walk down the hall. Teachers teach differently because they understand the individualistic nature of learners and accept responsibility for teaching each and every student; they expect to work together and to be celebrated for doing so. Teachers talk about the positive aspects of their students and the learning environment. Administrators cannot wait to show off the great teaching and learning occurring in classrooms. Parents, students, teachers, administrators, staff, and community recognize that there is no mystery in being an inclusive school; it simply requires valuing students' individual strengths and ensuring a positive future for all learners. In making decisions throughout the day and year, the slogans "fair is not always equal" and "everyone gets what they need" are reflected in the positive way each and every child is accepted, embraced, valued, nurtured, and respected.

Demystifying inclusion at the secondary level is an ever-present challenge. I believe the real solution to inclusive education occurs only when administrators, teachers, staff, families, and communities are empowered and truly believe they can make a difference. I have yet to encounter a school that has come to the end of the journey related to successful inclusive education. Rather, inclusion is a dynamic process that must be consistent enough for everyone to understand the mission, yet flexible enough to meet the unique needs and gifts of each child who walks into the school. Inclusion is not an end in itself; rather it is the beginning of a never-ending journey of challenges and celebrations on the way to ensuring the successful growth and education of each and every child.

Chapter 1

Creating a School-Wide Inclusive Culture

In schools that create inclusive climates, all children feel safe being who they are; they are assured that each and every teacher in each and every subject area will meet their needs to the greatest extent possible. Classrooms are orderly (I did not say quiet, but orderly) and the focus is on each student feeling comfortable and safe to take risks in order to grow as a learner (Lieber et al., 2000; Palmer, 2005). Conflict may exist between teachers or students, but it is the exception instead of the rule. Development of such safe havens is critical for all students, especially for those with disabilities.

For inclusion to be embraced as a reality as well as a philosophy, change must occur across many aspects of the school. Although these changes can be as simple as assigning students to a great teacher or creating a great classroom climate, (Titone, 2005), an inclusive environment is easier to develop when some basic practices are in place within the entire school structure and there is a sense of consistency in areas such as discipline, grading, and social skills instruction. The pages that follow offer examples of effective practices that help create and maintain inclusive schools where teachers expect to meet the needs of a wider range of learners. With school-wide, proactive planning to meet the needs of a diverse set of learners who may have a broad spectrum of needs, inclusion at the secondary level is more successful. In these schools, inclusion is a never-ending, constantly changing, dynamic process that ensures that students with learning, behavioral, or sensory disabilities are successful alongside their non-disabled peers (Villa, Thousand, Nevin & Liston, A. 2005).

A single teacher cannot simply *do things* to make a school inclusive. Rather, the process of inclusion starts with the belief of a teacher or amongst the staff that all students can learn, albeit in different ways and at different rates, and that students with disabilities should therefore be included in general education classrooms with their non-disabled peers (Hitchcock, Meyer, Rose & Jackson, 2002; Pivik, Mccomas & Laflamme, 2002). Furthermore, in order to facilitate successful inclusion educators must have the conviction that learning encompasses more than just academics. The inclusive classroom values the growth and development of the whole student, including social and emotional skills that are so critical during adolescent years.

More often than not, failure at inclusion is the result of ineffective instruction rather than poor learning. In his work on urban pedagogy, Dr. Martin Haberman argues that good teaching must occur in all schools and that good teaching is what learners in urban schools need in order to succeed. Similarly, I would argue that if students with disabilities are to survive in secondary schools, they need great teaching that embraces the full range of learning and/or behavioral needs presented by today's students (Fennick & Liddy, 2001; Hardin & Hardin, 2002). There need not be a special education pedagogy, but rather all teachers should adopt an approach that accommodates many different kinds of learners in their classrooms.

In order for students to be included in the general education curriculum, teachers must modify their instruction to meet students' needs rather than expecting students to change how they learn. In creating lessons with the assumption of a population of learners that includes students who are blind, deaf, those with special behavioral needs, as well as those who may not talk and/or walk, teachers reflect the philosophy of Universal Design for Learning (UDL), a topic that will be covered more fully in Chapter 3. Lessons that are initially designed to incorporate the needs of students with disabilities and a range of learners will not require as much adaptation in the future. Lessons such as these not only meet the needs of students with disabilities, but also provide maximum opportunity for the unique learning styles of all students at the secondary level.

While inclusion is increasingly embraced by educators, many are still skeptical about this delivery service model. People often challenge inclusion by saying that it is just a trend and that in time we will decide to return students with special needs to more restrictive settings. I immediately respond to this issue by referring to history. Although the field of special education has had bumps in the road and at times has taken two steps forward followed by two steps back, continued progress has been made in giving students with disabilities more rights and integrating them more fully into society. For instance, just fifty years ago a student whose learning was too delayed or behavior too challenging was not even allowed to attend public school (Kavale & Forness, 2000). Today, however, denying a child access to the general education curriculum and public education is the greatest exception where it was formerly the norm (Weiner, 2003; Simpson, 2004; Bloomfield & Cooper, 2003).

As we move towards increased integration of students with disabilities into general education settings, we have to realize that inclusion is a foreign concept for some educators, taking them into uncharted territory both personally and professionally. With the exception of those embarking on teaching in the recent past, many of today's teachers were not initially trained in the model of inclusion. Few were educated alongside children with disabilities, and few expected to experience inclusion when entering teaching (Dixon, 2005; Schulte, Osborne & Erchul, 1993).

Until recently, our teacher preparation programs had not been successful in preparing secondary teachers to work effectively with students with disabilities (Nougaret, Scruggs & Mastropieri, 2005; Resta, Askins & Huling, 1999; Kent, 2005). Thus, most teachers were not prepared, either personally or professionally, to work effectively with students with disabilities at the secondary level. Pre-service programs still exist today that do not even require secondary educators to take courses about students with disabilities.

While there are teachers in today's workforce who are well prepared to teach content to kids who are eager, willing and able to learn, many of these same teachers are unequipped for today's classroom of students whose needs range so greatly and who may not be overly interested in the content being taught. Until we have teachers who have been educated alongside students with disabilities and are prepared to work with them, we will continue to face challenges in embracing a philosophy of inclusion where people believe that students with disabilities belong in general education classrooms - the very heart of inclusive education. Stated most simply, we still face a generation gap in our teaching force.

Inclusive Philosophy

A shared vision of inclusion emerges in different ways at different schools. In some cases, the philosophy is shaped and driven by administration. Yet in other schools a teacher or a small group of teachers embraces inclusion and begins to spread positive energy across the school. No matter how this vision emerges, the bottom line is that strong inclusive schools must develop and share a philosophy about educating students with disabilities. Inclusive schools are constantly focused on ensuring that students remain in the more inclusive general education setting.

In the best case scenario, an inclusive philosophy is embraced not only by a teacher or a team or even a single school. Rather, it is present throughout the entire community, among members of the school board, and in other schools within the district. Everyone is educated about this philosophy and what they can do to help ensure the success of all students. When outsiders visit these schools, administration, faculty, staff, and students are able to articulate their commitment to inclusive education of all students. More importantly, an outsider can see inclusion in action within a few minutes of being in a school or on campus (Larson, 2005; Boscardin, 2005).

There are times when the adage "seeing is believing" can be most effective in providing an impetus for the development of a shared philosophy. This visual image is particularly helpful when there is resistance among administrators, parents, or teachers. Arrange for a visit to a school where inclusion is flourishing, or at least is operational. Observe first hand: see what it looks like. When possible, try to find someone in the same curricular content area who embraces the philosophy of inclusion. Be prepared to ask questions and listen carefully. Be mindful that there may not be answers to all of your questions, but there may be suggestions that can be incorporated as you create the inclusive philosophy of your own school.

In inclusive schools students expect that their classes will have a diverse learning population, and as citizens of this learning community they expect that they will help each other. Teachers also expect that they will serve all students. When a student fails, it is not the student alone who fails but also the teacher who failed to meet the student's needs. The education of students with disabilities is not just on the shoulders of the special educator; rather, all educators take ownership for the learning of all students.

Consistent School-Wide Practices

A hallmark of inclusive schools is consistency of practices. Optimally, this consistency extends across an entire district, but sometimes we need to be satisfied with having it only within a particular school or even a classroom as a start. Yet remember, if inclusion is embraced in only one classroom or one school, then the child may wind up the victim of a disjointed education, one that changes as the philosophy of the teacher or school changes (Dieker, 2001).

Fairness

One of the most important practices at the core of an inclusive school relates to the concept of fairness and what constitutes fairness. Fairness means that all students will get what they need. This definition may make things look different and unbalanced according to our current paradigm, but it is the basis for ensuring that all students have their individual needs met through a process that carefully assesses what they need in order to be safe and successful. Stated differently, *fairness is not sameness*. This issue has to be addressed not only with students but with the entire school community: all general and special education staff, including all support and clerical staff who interact with the students in any way and, of course, parents and families. It is especially critical for co-teachers to have a mutual understanding and agreement on the definition of fairness. The premise that fairness is not sameness must become part of the school-wide culture and part of the culture of every inclusive classroom. Above all, in inclusive schools fairness is not open for negotiation.

The concept of fairness is not simple, nor is it easily understood. One way to explain it to students is to use the example of the Heimlich maneuver. Specifically, if only one person is choking it is not fair to administer the maneuver to everyone present, but rather only to the one person who needs it. This same type of logic can be used when students say it is not "fair" when one student gets something and another does not.

Another way to address the issue of fairness at the classroom level is through the following activity that can be undertaken during the first week of school. I like to call it "doctor's prescription." For this activity, the teacher comes to class dressed in doctor's scrubs and a stethoscope. The class begins with the teacher asking each student to think of an illness that they could have. Then, as each student states his or her illness, the teacher gives the same advice: "Take two aspirins and call me in the morning." At first the students laugh, but by the time the teacher has given the same prescription to all thirty students they begin to think of this response as ridiculous which, of course, is the intended outcome. Once all illnesses have been disclosed and all students provided with the same treatment, the teacher can use this activity to talk about the diversity of students in the classroom and their varied, individual needs.

Following the "doctor's prescription" exercise, the teacher shares the definition of fairness: everyone gets what he or she needs. The teacher then explains that if one student goes to the doctor because of a cold, and another student goes due to a broken arm, each would expect individualized treatment from the doctor. The same is true in a school. Students are reminded that although they may be similar in age, they are different in what they need to be successful learners. A student who needs extensive help with reading may be very good at writing, or vice versa. The teacher typically ends this discussion by creating a large prescription pad that has a definition of fairness (see Exhibit 1.1). Thereafter, when one student gets a calculator during math class and another student claims this is not fair, the teacher simply refers to the prescription for learning related to fairness, and reiterates that each student will be prescribed specifically what he or she needs.

Positive Behavioral Intervention Supports (PBIS)

In strong secondary inclusive schools, everyone is clear about what is expected from students, and students know that the rules are consistent from class to class. Using models such as Positive Behavioral Intervention Supports (see Exhibit 1.2 for basic information on PBIS, or www.pbis.org), students with behavioral or social issues do not have to wonder about the rules in each classroom. Take, for instance, a typical middle or high school where each teacher sets his or her own rules. Students with behavioral challenges must not only focus on the academic demands, but also must exert effort trying to conform to rules that may vary from class to class. In a strong inclusive school that uses a model such as PBIS, staff members agree in advance on issues that the teachers will attempt to resolve, and identify other specific behaviors that may become the responsibility of the administrators to resolve. For example, if the consequence for a student using a disrespectful tone with a teacher is a phone call home in one classroom, that same consequence would apply in each and every classroom. If a student uses profanity with a teacher, the rule may be that this student is sent to the office. In this case, the student knows in advance that using profanity in any teacher's classroom will result in being sent to the office. However, in schools that employ PBIS, the focus is not on consequences for bad behavior as much as on rewarding students' positive behavior.

Exhibit 1.2 ~ Positive Behavioral Supports: Definition from Website

In a school-wide approach to PBIS...

> the emphasis is on school-wide systems of support that include proactive strategies for defining, teaching, and supporting appropriate student behaviors to create positive school environments. Instead of using a patchwork of individual behavioral management plans, a continuum of positive behavior support for all students within a school is implemented in areas including in the classroom and outside of classroom settings (such as hallways, restrooms). Positive behavior support is an application of a behaviorally based systems approach to enhance the capacity of schools, families, and communities to design effective environments that improve the link between research-validated practices and the environments in which teaching and learning occurs. Attention is focused on creating and sustaining primary (school-wide), secondary(classroom), and tertiary (individual) systems of support that improve lifestyle results (personal, health, social, family, work, recreation) for all children and youth by making problem behavior less effective, efficient, and relevant, and desired behavior more functional.

The utilization of PBIS supports the implementation and operation of strong inclusive secondary schools. Such schools exhibit the following:

- Rules are consistent from class to class so that teachers and students no longer have to spend time or energy determining rules or consequences on a case-by-case basis.
- Students are acknowledged and rewarded for positive behaviors instead of only being acknowledged or punished for negative behavior.
- Teachers in co-teaching classrooms agree upon rules and consequences before they begin working together, saving time and energy in building a collaborative environment.
- Students are taught social skills in inclusive settings so that they understand appropriate expectations. These skills are not from a generic curriculum but are derived from behavioral standards identified within the school.
- A continuum of support is provided for dealing with students' behavioral needs, acknowledging that a "one size

fits all" approach may not work for some students with behavioral disabilities. This continuum of support parallels the continuum of services in IDEA.

• Data is at the core of decision-making. Changes are based on collective, school-wide data related to a student's behavior and not merely on one teacher's thoughts and observations. This type of collection follows the current focus on determining services based on Response to Intervention. See Chapter 7 for more information on RTI.

Just as there is consistency in dealing with problematic behavior in a strong inclusive school, there is the same consistency in celebrating good behavior. Teachers find unique ways to celebrate the positive behaviors that occur in their classrooms. For example, instead of only punishing students for being tardy, a teacher may decide to randomly reward all students who come to class on time. In a strong school, a genuine strengths-based approach is embraced so that less attention is given to the negative behaviors. More about the topic of celebrating strengths is provided in Chapter 2.

School-wide consistency is especially critical when co-teaching is occurring. If a school does not have a consistent system, special education teachers may chose to deal with behavior differently than their general education counterparts. In co-teaching situations, the two teachers must talk in advance about their behavioral philosophies. However, preplanning time can be greatly reduced for co-teachers if this discussion has already happened on a school-wide level and consistency of procedures exists. When co-teachers start to work together in a school that has developed a consistent system, they need only reaffirm their commitment to this school-wide system for behavior.

The dynamics of classes at the secondary level change from hour to hour. Answers to the following questions can be used to help develop a classroom that is more accepting of students with a range of educational and behavioral needs (modified from Maas, 1989). They will assist teachers in developing responses to behavioral issues in classrooms across the building and will also help in the development of a climate that is supportive of students with disabilities.

- Are consistent classroom rules established and posted across the team or throughout the school?
- Is there a system to ensure that students receive more positive than negative feedback?
- Do seating charts meet the needs of students with disabilities as well as their non-disabled peers to ensure positive learning outcomes?
- Is there a system related to out-of-classroom passes (e.g., a place for students to log their twice a week pass from the class)?
- Is there a consistent make-up policy across the team or school that is posted for students?
- Are there identified strategies that will be used to ensure students' self-esteem is not damaged?
- Is there a system to allow students to know their progress on at least a weekly basis?
- Are the rules and consequences clear enough that all misbehavior can be dealt with in less than three seconds?
- Are issues that can be negotiated (e.g., date to turn in homework) and those that cannot be (e.g., having more than two passes a week) clear to the students?
- Are all posted rules presented at a reading level and language usage level that is student friendly?
- Are there defined ways to utilize proximity control to manage behavior?

Dealing with Negative Behaviors

Strong inclusive schools recognize that there is a full continuum of services available to students under the law, and that at times placement in a more restrictive setting is in a particular student's best interest; for no matter how well schools implement inclusive practices, they are not immune from the extreme behavioral issues of some students. A core principle of PBIS is that there will always be a small percentage of students for whom this model of consistency will not be sufficient. A need may exist to create levels of environments to assist and protect both the student with a disability and his or her non-disabled peers.

The difference between utilizing more exclusionary settings in inclusive environments versus traditional, non-inclusive environments is the school's philosophical approach. In accord with the philosophy of inclusion, teachers do not celebrate when a student's behavior is so extreme that he or she has to be removed from the general education setting. Instead, they mourn the loss of the student they are not able to serve, clearly define the behavior that caused the removal to a more restrictive environment, and immediately develop a plan as to what can be done to return the student to the most inclusive environment possible. In inclusive schools teachers and/or teacher assistance teams do not immediately refer out for services; instead, they explore how they can deliver specialized services to students with severe behavioral needs in the general education setting. To do so, they may consider the questions posed in Exhibit 1.3. By answering these questions, the staff can use specific, observable information to work on a strengths-based approach.

Exhibit 1.3 ~ Worksheet for Discussing Inclusive Behaviors

Prior to presenting a student to the teacher assistance team or talking with a colleague about a student, the teacher should complete each of the boxes provided below. This information will provide for a more productive meeting by ensuring the focus is on the specific troublesome behavior while also making note of the student's positive behavior in the classroom.

Student's Name _____ **Teacher's Name** _____ **Date** _____

What does the student consistently do that bothers me or his/her peers?	
How do I respond? How do his/her peer respond?	
What is the student trying to tell me by acting out?	
What does this student do that is positive?	
How can I and the student's peers provide support for these positive behaviors?	
What do I like the most about this student?	

Another common practice I have observed in strong inclusive schools is teacher-to-teacher support for behavioral challenges. For example, in one school, before a teacher can request a meeting about a student's behavior, that teacher must ask a trusted colleague to observe the specific student for a minimum of five minutes in the classroom (see Exhibit 1.4A). Of course, most observations last longer than five minutes, but this time frame seems realistic for even the busiest teachers. The teacher asks the peer to observe the student, using a simple ABC chart (See Exhibit 1.4B). The peer then shares his or her brief observation with the teacher. Teachers who use this system report that sometimes an observation and a few suggestions from a peer are sufficient to address the problem and a team conference is no longer needed. However, if more intervention is warranted, the teacher with the concern can then use this chart when presenting the student to the student support/school-based team.

Peers doing the observing in such scenarios frequently report that they learn something about their own teaching through this process. This type of collaborative support is critical in inclusive schools. Teachers make over 1,300 decisions a day and rarely have time to dissect each and every one. An objective view is therefore extremely valuable. Also, as hard as it is to admit, teachers are human. There will frequently be at least one student who presents challenges on a daily basis or who the teacher may not be overly excited to teach. Through peer observation teachers are reminded of Dewey's philosophy: "Look not for fault in the child, but in the teaching of the child" (Dewey, 1933). Accordingly, in strong inclusive schools that is precisely what occurs. The teacher takes ownership for creating an environment that fosters positive behaviors and also assumes ownership when misbehavior occurs.

Exhibit 1.4A ~ Peer Observation Form: Introduction

Part A of this form is to be completed by the teacher who is requesting to be observed. It is given to the peer so that the specific issues of concern can be observed.

The student I would like for you to observe is _____
and he/she is most often seated _____

The specific behavior(s) about which I am most concerned is (are)_____
_____

Name: _____ Date:_____

Exhibit 1.4 ~ Peer Observation Form: Feedback

Part B of the form is to be completed by the peer who is doing the observing. The comments should relate to the areas of concern as noted by the teacher in Part A.

Time Observed	Antecedent	Behavior	Consequence

General Observations/Reflections _____
_____
_____

Suggestions or strategies to consider _____
_____
_____

Name: _____ Date:_____

Criteria for Inclusion and Exclusion

Have you ever thought about the life of children with disabilities? The tests and criteria that are used to define many mild disabilities are so subjective in nature that, unless the students are at very low levels of functioning, their placement may change not by their skill level but by the state, county, city, school or classroom in which they are educated. Being in the field of special education literally all my life, I would love to say with certainty that we can test children and reliably determine if they have a learning disability, behavioral disorder or other disability. However, in reality, simply moving across a state line can change a student's label, placement or even eligibility for services in the field of special education. Even within the same city, moving from one school to another can change where and how a student receives services (resource, self-contained or general education setting), this change perhaps being dictated by nothing more than the philosophy of the staff or the historical model that is in place—otherwise expressed as the *"this is the way we have always done it"* mentality.

A huge catalyst for change in the service delivery model for students with disabilities has been the *No Child Left Behind Act (NCLB)* as well as the parallel reauthorization of the *Individuals with Disabilities Education Improvement Act (IDEIA)* of 2004. The repercussions of these laws on the secondary teacher are both positive and negative, and can be confusing and unsettling. Strong language in IDEA '04 states that the primary teacher of record must be certified in the content area that he or she is teaching. This presents a problem when the special education teacher has a student in a self-contained or resource setting. Many secondary special education teachers who are amazing educators and have committed their lives to improving the world for children with disabilities are subject to a mandate that says they are not qualified to provide content area instruction. At the same, time this change has been positive in that it provides students with disabilities access to teachers who have specialized knowledge and skills for content area courses. This dual outcome, of course, is a mixed blessing because in the past, many students with disabilities have not had the same opportunities or curricular experiences as their non-disabled peers. This reality is just one more issue arising from the currently disjointed system of service delivery caused by the lack of integration between general education and special education (Dieker, 2001).

How does this scenario affect students with disabilities in our school settings? The law clearly states that students with disabilities are to have access to highly qualified teachers and to the general education setting. Realistically, however, teachers, students and parents may at times need to explore alternative placements, especially as students go through the stages of adolescence wherein some problems can become exacerbated. The law has always embraced a continuum of services, and I continue to believe it always will. It must be recognized and validated that the decisions for placement are critical in the life of a student. Such decisions must therefore be made with full knowledge of the range of available services, and the pros and cons of each for that student at that specific time in his or her life. It is thus important to carefully and mindfully review student placement on a regular basis. Full inclusion may not be the answer for every student, but it can most certainly be the goal.

The materials that follow in Exhibit 1.5 outline the continuum of services from the most restrictive at the top to the least restrictive at the bottom. As noted in the reference, these options have existed since 1962 and will probably continue to exist under various names for many years to come.

Exhibit 1.5 ~ Continuum of Placement Options for Students with Disabilities

- hospital and/or institutional setting
- residential school
- special day school
- full-time special class
- general education classroom plus resource room service
- general education classroom with supplementary instruction or treatment
- general education classroom with consultation
- general education setting

Adapted from Exceptional Children, Vol. 28, No. 7, March, 1962, p. 368.

Although this continuum has been in place for over forty years, its use in some schools at the secondary level has been limited. Many times, placement of students is based more on exclusion criteria, often in the absence of clear inclusion criteria. For example, schools frequently have policies to exclude students who are physically violent toward others. Exclusion might also be based simply on the label given to the student. But strong inclusive schools adopt parallel criteria for students to be included. Consider the following examples:

- One school's policy states that if a student who is labeled Emotional/Behavior Disorder (E/BD), touches another student inappropriately, he or she is to be moved to a more exclusionary setting for at least five days (this type of structure having been discussed at IEP meetings at which parents were made aware of policies and procedures). After five days the student is returned to the general education classroom with some supports, provided there is not a reason to believe the student's potentially dangerous behavior will continue (e.g., if the student continues to have violent episodes then the team will keep the child in the more exclusionary setting and continue to revisit placement regularly).

- In another school, students who need reading instruction (because they scored below the state standard) may be pulled out of the general education classroom for a reading class. However, this additional class is scheduled as an elective so that the students do not miss their general education reading instruction. In addition, every four weeks a reading assessment is conducted and once students reach grade level criteria they nolonger continue in the self-contained reading model.
- In yet another school, the criteria states that if students need to be removed from the general education setting because of a specific incident, they are to be placed back in the general education setting within six weeks. When students are removed, a specific criterion is provided by the general education teacher (and again shared with parents and made part of the legal IEP process) detailing what specifically the student needs to learn/do to return to the general education setting.

In a school where teachers expect and want students to return to the general education setting, the criteria for inclusion permeates the thinking and actions of teachers, students, and their families.

Preparing the Student with Disabilities for Inclusion

An important consideration prior to starting an inclusive plan is the preparation of students for a more inclusive setting. Often schools spend a great deal of time getting teachers ready for inclusion but do not consider how to promote acceptance of these students' unique social, behavioral and instructional needs among students. It is important to ensure that students in special education are ready for the greater, or at least different, demands of the general education classroom.

In a study my colleagues and I conducted, we observed successfully and unsuccessfully included middle school students and then developed role-play scenarios to assist in preparing students for inclusion in the general education setting (Monda-Amaya, Dieker & Reed, 1998). Subsequent to the students' involvement in the role-plays, they visited the general education setting and shared their specific concerns as well as the goals they felt they needed to meet in order to be successfully included in that general education setting. We learned that students feared things that we as adults might not consider, such as not knowing the students in the class, the teacher's sense of humor, and how to ask for help. We then took their concerns and set corresponding daily goals.

This role-playing technique has been utilized and expanded upon in many classrooms. Teams or grade levels benefit from creating criteria for multiple categories, such as those set forth in Exhibit 1.6. Using this form, the special education teacher identifies the skills needed for success in the general education classroom. These skills are then taught to the entire class and each student sets goals on a form, as presented in Exhibit 1.7. One team even went so far as to count the mastery of these skills as 10% of the final grade, not just for students with disabilities, but for all students in the class.

Exhibit 1.6 ~ General Education Skills

(To be completed by the special education teacher as a reflection of needs in the general education class.)

What skills in each of the areas listed below must students in your class master in order to be successful in the general education setting?

Behavior_____

Attitude_____

Organization_____

Before Class_____

During Class_____

After Class_____

Group Work_____

Exhibit 1.7 ~ Daily Goals Sheets

(to be completed by each student)

Student Name _____ Date _____

Daily Goal	Mon	Tues	Wed	Thur	Fri
Goal 1	1 2 3 4 5	1 2 3 4 5	1 2 3 4 5	1 2 3 4 5	1 2 3 4 5
Goal 2	1 2 3 4 5	1 2 3 4 5	1 2 3 4 5	1 2 3 4 5	1 2 3 4 5
Goal 3	1 2 3 4 5	1 2 3 4 5	1 2 3 4 5	1 2 3 4 5	1 2 3 4 5
Notes					

1 — I did not meet   5 — I met expectations completely

The importance of social skills instruction for all students is easily understood at the adolescent level, as is the need to ensure acceptance of students by their peers. Strong inclusive schools operate under a holistic approach to inclusion, one that encompasses all students. Schools that have evolved as inclusive schools understand that students with disabilities need not always be tracked into lower level classes.

Advanced Placement (AP) classes often provide excellent environments for embracing diverse learners. One school decided to move towards a more inclusive environment by placing students with behavioral needs in AP classes in which there were rarely behavioral issues. This environment provided strong models of behavior as well as academically appropriate settings for students who had the potential to learn but whose behavior often impacted their learning. Despite some strong doubts by teachers in the school it soon became clear that behavioral issues were minimized when these students with the label of emotional/

behavioral disorders were challenged in AP classes. The opposite outcome is often observed when students are tracked into lower level courses.

No matter how you go about it in your school or district, criteria must exist for inclusion and, in extreme cases and only when absolutely necessary, there must also be a process to access more exclusionary services. Inclusive schools are set apart by their focus on what students need to function successfully in the general education setting instead of only detailing how and when they are to be removed. Additionally, in developing strong, inclusive secondary schools, everyone must understand the impact of a change in the method of service delivery. Teachers, staff, parents and most importantly students, must be provided with the opportunity to develop the understanding and skills that are necessary to make inclusion work. In inclusive schools, consistency is one key to success, but even more important is a community of administrators, teachers, staff, students and families that believes that together they can successfully meet the needs of all students in the general education setting to the maximum extent appropriate. This sense of community and strong philosophical underpinning constitutes an inclusive culture.

Reflective Questions

1. What is the philosophy of our school?
2. How does our school deal consistently with
    a. behavior,
    b. service delivery options,
    c. learning environment?
3. How is the concept of fairness incorporated by administration, teachers, students, parents, and the community?
4. What is being done at our school to ensure that students are ready for more inclusive environments?
5. How can we instigate changes in our school climate? Make a list and pick one way to work on this issue immediately.

References

Bloomfield, D. C., & Cooper, B. S. (2003). Making sense of NCLB. *T.H.E. Journal, 30*(10), 6-32.

Boscardin, M. L. (2005). The administrative role in transforming secondary schools to support inclusive evidence-based practices. *American Secondary Education, 33*(3), 21-32.

Dewey, J. (1933). *How we think.* Boston: D.C. Heath.

Dieker, L. A. (2001). Collaboration as a tool to resolve the issue of disjointed service delivery. *Journal of Educational and Psychological Consultation, 12,* 263-269.

Dixon, S. (2005). Inclusion - not segregation or integration is where a student with special needs belongs. *Journal of Educational Thought, 39*(1), 33-53.

Farlow, L. (1996). A quartet of success stories: How to make inclusion work. *Educational Leadership, 53*(fall), 51-55.

Fennick, R., & Liddy, D. (2001). Responsibilities and preparation for collaborative teaching: Co-teachers' perspectives. *Teacher Education and Special Education, 24*(3), 229-240.

Haberman, M. (2005). *Star teachers of children of poverty.* Haberman Educational Foundation, Houston, TX.

Hardin, B., & Hardin, M. (2002). Into the mainstream: Practical strategies for teaching in inclusive environments. *The*

Clearing House, 75(4), 175-178.

Lieber, J., Hanson, M. J., Beckman, P. J., Odom, S. L., Sandall, S. R., Schwartz, I. S., et al. (2000). Key influences on the initiation and implementation of inclusive preschool programs. *Exceptional Children, 67*(1), 83-98.

Hitchcock, C., Meyer, A., Rose, D., & Jackson, R. (2002). Providing new access to the general curriculum: Universal design for learning. *Teaching Exceptional Children, 35*(2), 8-17.

Kavale, K. A., & Forness, S. R. (2000). History, rhetoric, and reality: Analysis of the inclusion debate. *Remedial and Special Education, 21*(5), 279-296.

Kent, A. M. (2005). Acknowledging the need facing teacher preparation programs: Responding to make a difference. *Education, 25*(3), 343-348.

Larson, N. W. (2005). "The time has come," the walrus said, "to speak of many things!" *Learning Disability Quarterly, 28*(4), 247-248.

Maas, D. (1989). Inspiring Active Learning. Unpublished handbook.

Monda-Amaya, L., Dieker, L., & Reed, F. (1998). Preparing students with learning disabilities to participate in inclusive classrooms. *Learning Disabilities Research and Practice, 13,* 169-182.

Nougaret, A. A., Scruggs, T. E., & Mastropieri, M. A. (2005). Does teacher education produce better special education teachers? *Exceptional Children, 71*(3), 217-229.

Palmer, R. J. (2005). Meeting diverse needs. *Kappa Delta Pi Record, 41*(2), 56-91.

Pivik, J., Mccomas, J., & Laflamme, M. (2002). Barriers and facilitators to inclusive education. *Exceptional Children, 69*(1), 97-107.

Resta, V., Askins, B. E., & Huling, L. (1999). Issues in secondary teacher preparation. *The Teacher Educator, 35*(1), 57-67.

Schulte, A. C., Osborne, S. S., & Erchul, W. P. (1998). Effective special education: A united states dilemma. *School Psychology Review, 27*(1).

Simpson, R. L. (2004). Inclusion of students with behavior disorders in general education settings: Research and measurement issues. *Behavioral Disorders, 30*(1), 19-31.

Titone, C. (2005). The philosophy of inclusion: Roadblocks and remedies for the teacher and the teacher educator. *Journal* of *Educational Thought, 39*(1), 7-32.

Villa, R. A., Thousand, J. S., Nevin, A., & Liston, A. (2005). Successful inclusive practices in middle and secondary schools. *American Secondary Education, 33*(3), 33-50.

Weiner, H. M. (2003). Effective inclusion: Professional development in the context of the classroom. *Teaching Exceptional Children, 35*(6), 12-18.

Chapter 2

Celebrating the Success of All Students

In strong inclusive schools, all students are celebrated in all aspects of learning and life. Resources and rewards are not taken away from high performing students, but structures, ceremonies, and programs are added to embrace individualism as well as the progress of all learners in the school. Achievements are celebrated by encouraging teachers to creatively provide all students with opportunities to give and receive. In these inclusive schools, fairness is expected. A system of grading and assessment breaks from traditional modes to acknowledge the diversity of the learners in each and every class.

Celebrations of student learning can be found daily in schools that embrace an inclusive philosophy. My favorite example is from a school that did something very simple that made a huge impact on a student named Eddie. One day, Eddie, a student who was quite often in trouble, stopped me as I walked into the school. He said, "I did it! I did it!" With interest I responded, "You did what, Eddie?" Initially, I thought he said, "I made the honor roll and my name was in the paper last night." I proceeded to congratulate him on getting such good grades and say how impressed I was that he made the honor roll. Eddie quickly corrected my naïve thinking and said, "Lady, I ain't got good grades. I said I made the 'on-a-roll' list." Looking confused, I asked him to explain what the "on-a-roll" list was. He proceeded to give me a fifteen-minute explanation of the "on-a-roll" criteria. He informed me that most people did not know the specifics, but he knew that he made the list because he had not touched anyone inappropriately for an entire quarter. He ended this special conversation by telling me that his grandmother was so proud of him that she took the paper to the senior citizen center to show all her friends. She even bought him a new Play Station 2! This is a perfect example of a secondary school thinking differently. Eddie knew he probably would never get the grades needed to be on the honor roll, but he was celebrated just as much as the class valedictorian because he had succeeded in improving his behavior. This example demonstrates how applying a true strengths-based approach and philosophy within a school can benefit all students.

As seen in the above example, differences are celebrated in strong secondary schools. In these schools, rewards for honor students are not removed or devalued, but instead activities/events such as the "on-a-roll" list are incorporated to ensure all students have a chance to be celebrated. Celebrations have to be different in secondary schools than those in elementary schools, and must be appropriate for teenagers. These measures are taken to ensure that students with disabilities are acknowledged for what they add to our schools and celebrated for their unique talents.

Another approach that has been used to ensure the strengths of all students are celebrated is detailed in Exhibit 2.1. In this example, a middle school team sends a newsletter home at the beginning of each quarter. This publication not only provides parents with ideas about ways to celebrate learning, but also pro- vides a chance for parents to connect with their children over activities that take place outside of the school. By suggesting topics for parents to discuss with their children, the newsletter promotes communication between school and home. In addition, student artwork, poems, short stories, and interesting thoughts can be included in the quarterly newsletter, giving students who might not be recognized in traditional ways the chance to be celebrated in school.

Another great way to celebrate students is to look for alter- native methods for them to demonstrate what they have learned. For example, in one school, all assessments are based on state standards but allow students to use multiple ways to demonstrate they have mastered these standards. Students can create poems, plays, murals, or they can use any other way they choose to demonstrate mastery of the key points of the curriculum. This type of creative assessment not only makes adaptations and modifications easier, but is a great way to celebrate various types of learning. It also shows that everyone has gifts and encourages students to think about how to make use of their individual gifts. I also find that when teachers use exhibition assessment, students work much harder to prepare than they might for a more traditional assessment, and have fun along the way. More information on creative assessments can be found in Chapter 7.

In one secondary school, monthly student exhibitions are open to parents and family members. Minimal participation in parent-teacher conferences existed prior to introducing exhibitions, but the number of parents that turned out to see their children present exhibitions was amazing. Why? Because parents may not want to come to a traditional parent-teacher conference (especially if past experiences with these conferences have been negative) but they may be willing to come and see their child present his or her skills in a positive and celebratory format. In this school, students' work is grounded in community activities (e.g., helping a local gardener grow plants) and these "real life" skills are shared with their families. First, students take home the crops they grow. Second, during the exhibition, they use these real life experiences to show their command of math, science, social studies and English concepts.

Another unique way a school demonstrates its more inclusive approach is to celebrate all students by sending them to the principal's office for a unique reason. Many students at a young age learn that going to the principal's office is like going to the doctor – you usually only go there if something is wrong. This school decided that as more students were included, they needed ways to celebrate success. They incorporated the following activity with the goal of providing a more positive image of their principal's office. All teachers in this school are given postcards and when a student does something outstanding, teachers simply write the student's name on the card, along with a statement of the reason the student is being acknowledged, and the card is then forwarded to the office. Then, each day names on the cards are read over the loud speaker, calling students to the principal's office. When the students arrive, they are given a handshake by the assistant principal and asked to complete their parent/guardian's name and address on the front of the card. Then the school simply puts these postcards into the mail. A local business provides the cards and better yet, the cards are bright neon color so that in this community even the mail carrier knows when a positive note is sent home! Many parents in this community talk about how the mail carrier congratulates them on their son or daughter's behavior or academic achievement in school.

In traditional secondary schools, the same few students are honored repeatedly, whether at graduation ceremonies, athletic banquets, or other school functions. Parents whose children are celebrated are thrilled, whereas parents of children with disabilities attend such functions with the expectation that their child will not get an award and will feel disappointed. Parents of children with disabilities need to hear their children's names called at awards presentations. Even more importantly, the students themselves need to be recognized in front of their peers, especially in adolescence. In strong inclusive schools, children with disabilities are appreciated for their unique gifts (e.g., lots of energy, a big heart, a smile, a sense of humor).

One school addresses this issue by having monthly award ceremonies that include students' exhibits of what they have learned. These ceremonies serve multiple purposes and have some excellent benefits such as:

- Students work very hard on their exhibition performance because they are sharing it with their classmates as well as their parents.
- Parents get a glimpse of what students are learning in school (because we all know that adolescents rarely bring papers home and talk to their parents about school because it is just not cool).
- Teachers use this ceremonial time to make certain that children with unique gifts are rewarded throughout the semester.
- All students get to demonstrate their strengths which might not be reflected in a traditional letter grade system.
- Community is built among teachers, administrators, parents and students through these ceremonies.

All students are celebrated when new ways are added to acknowledge the unique gifts of each and every child while the more traditional ceremonies recognizing gifted and talented students continue to be valued.

The following story about celebrating under unique circumstances is truly exciting. It occurred in a high school where only four special education teachers strongly embraced an inclusive philosophy; unfortunately, the administration had mixed feelings about how to serve students with disabilities. These special education teachers really wanted to include their students in the general education setting and celebrate their attributes. They also knew they had to be truly creative so they started by offering all students a strategy class which was designed to help students on their SAT exams. However, in projecting an inclusive philosophy, they decided to have each test prep class of thirty students include eight to ten students with disabilities. Then, in a resource period, the students with disabilities were pre-taught the skills that were going to be covered the next day in the new strategy class. When class got underway, the "best and the brightest" in the school recognized that their classmates who were disabled already understood the strategies being taught. This, of course, is because they had learned them the previous day! The students with disabilities were even asked at times to lead the class on the strategies they already knew, thus demonstrating their strengths to the rest of the population. The students with disabilities became so respected as peers in the class, that soon the general education students were demanding that these students have more opportunities for inclusive courses. At this point the administration could no longer question the model as general education students could see the value of working with their peers with disabilities.

This college preparation course actually includes numerous learning strategies developed by the University of Kansas for students with disabilities (see www.ku-crl.org for information on these strategies). It has expanded and is now offered in several content areas, allowing students with special needs to be included. All of this occurred because of the vision of a team of teachers. This account demonstrates the ingenious way that teachers brought the general education setting to their students with disabilities. When it is difficult to work within the system, strategies such as this often allow teachers to work around the system. The outcome, no matter how it is accomplished, is to remain focused on the goal of providing students with disabilities the maximum opportunity to work with their non-disabled peers.

Yet another remarkable celebration took place in a school that examined its graduation rates for students with disabilities (a strategy I strongly recommend for all schools) and took full ownership of their failure. In this particular school, over ninety percent of students without disabilities went on to college while less than thirty percent of students with learning disabilities progressed to college. The staff immediately began to identify where and how they were failing to prepare students with disabilities for a college education. What they learned from interviewing former students with disabilities was:

- Those who attempted college failed because they did not know how to register with the accessibility office at their colleges.
- Others did not clearly understand their disability well enough to ask for accommodations on the SAT or in specific classes.
- Some believed they could not take college entrance type exams.

However, the staff also learned and were able to celebrate the fact that upon completion of the intervention that is described in the subsequent paragraphs, the rate of students with learning disabilities who attended college rose to over eighty percent.

Self-Advocacy

Armed with the shockingly poor results from the examination of graduation rates, these teachers used this data to develop a new college preparation module for students with learning disabilities. This actually became a self-advocacy training session that was provided two days before school started, with a goal of teaching students about their areas of strength and weakness, and providing instruction on the skills needed to attend college. Through this training students:

- Learned about their own IQ and achievement test scores so they could understand their areas of strengths and weakness;
- Became familiar with their current Individualized Education Plans;
- Viewed videos about learning disabilities (*FAT City— Frustration, Anxiety, and Tension,* by Rick Lavoie);
- Learned tools to help them with specific areas of weakness;
- Used laughter as a component of learning, teaching students to laugh at themselves and to develop skills to handle issues with humor as appropriate;
- Wrote letters to the teachers of the classes for which they need accommodations;
- Learned to celebrate and embrace their differences instead of wondering why they struggled the way they did in certain areas.

During the first week of classes, each student was expected to make an appointment with his or her teachers to talk over any accommodations needed for that specific class. Students also gave their teachers the letters they had written regarding their learning disabilities during the training sessions. Exhibit 2.2 is a sample of one of these letters.

Exhibit 2.2

Dear Mr. B.,

     I am a sophomore in your sixth hour social studies class this semester. I am a student who works very hard and I am excited to be in your class. I also am a student who has been diagnosed with a learning disability. Basically, a learning disability means that I am like the rest of the students in my class but that somehow the wiring in my brain gets crossed when I try to write formal papers. The professionals tell me I have a writing processing problem. Basically what this means is that I can tell you what you want to know, but when I am asked to write a response I have difficulty getting my brain and hand to share what I know.

     On my individualized education plan, by law, it states that I can take my test in another setting. For your class, I am asking that if you give a social studies test that has any essay questions, I be allowed to go to the computer lab to write my responses. I also may at times use voice software to speak my response instead of typing it on my own. I think you will find I have pretty good thoughts if I can just put them into the computer in a different way and have more time.

I really like social studies and am excited to be in your class. If you have any questions about my needed accommodations, please see me the first two weeks of class. I too will make an appointment with you if you want to talk over how I learn best. Thank you for taking the time to read my letter and for helping me learn the way I can be successful.

Sincerely,
Zobee Keller

The necessity for students to learn about their strengths and how they can compensate for their disabilities is important at all levels of schooling, but is essential at the secondary level. Secondary students' understanding of their disabilities and skills in self-advocacy must be in collaboration with their parents/guardians, as they are an integral part of the educational team in strong secondary schools. In this particular letter, Zobee uses his self-advocacy skills in his high school classroom, knowing he will also be able to utilize these skills in college and beyond. Moreover, in the world of inclusive districts, self-advocacy is not something first taught at the secondary level. Instead, even middle school professionals expect students to come to their school knowing about their abilities and disabilities.

Self-advocacy skills are necessary for success in all phases of life and should be an integral part of the educational process in strong inclusive districts. I speak about this issue both as an educator and as a parent of a child with a disability. Our son was recently diagnosed with Tourette Syndrome and he knows more about this condition and his educational plan than most educators, nurses, and even pediatricians we have met.

Why are self-advocacy skills so critical, especially at the secondary level? In a typical secondary setting, schedules change at the last minute and the number of students that a special educator has to serve seems to increase with grade levels. If students are not taught to advocate for themselves, there is no way of ensuring their needs are met until either the special educator steps in to rescue them, the general educator realizes they are in crisis and seeks out information, or parents/guardians become angry because of failing grades and a perception that the school is not meeting their children's needs.

How do self-advocacy programs help in this situation? First, putting in place a self-advocacy program allows students to learn about their abilities and disabilities and to be better prepared for changing schedules, transitioning from school to school, attending college or securing employment. Currently, the number of students with disabilities who drop out of school is high, and the number of these students who enroll in college is much lower than that of their non-disabled peers. The reasons students drop out or do not attend college are multifaceted, but I do believe there is a direct correlation with these students not clearly understanding their abilities and disabilities and how they can receive support in high school as well as in college.

I believe all secondary teachers (especially special educators) should visit the accessibility offices of their local community and four-year colleges to learn what services are available to support students with disabilities in college. As a faculty member who has recruited several students with disabilities and worked with freshman who have disabilities, I am amazed at how many of these students come to college unaware of their disabilities, or in some cases unwilling to accept their need for some type of support. They start their freshman year in college without having registered with the accessibility office on their campus and then, at the end of the first semester, often cry foul play when their overall grade point average is a dismal 1.9 or less, or they actually fail. Consider what it takes to raise a 1.9 GPA to a 2.5, or higher, which is needed for most licensed professions. Beyond a miracle with lots of straight A's in future semesters, there is a limited chance of successful completion of a degree in many fields. Typically, this scenario plays out with the student giving up and dropping out of college.

Let's take that same scenario where the student, in this case Zobee, has been in an inclusive secondary setting and has been taught appropriate self-advocacy skills. He clearly understands all about his disability as well as how to ask for the support he needs. He has been through a program that taught him how to write a letter to his teacher and how to speak to each teacher about his disability. This student still sees college as a challenge but also knows which classes he will need support in as well as which subjects are his strongest and may make for a good major.

Although Zobee may still struggle in college, his chances for success have increased dramatically, not because his disability has been fixed, or he has received a miracle education that will erase all of his needs, but simply because he understands his needs and has been taught how to effectively advocate for himself. Zobee had learned basic advocacy skills related to his learning needs in elementary school, and in middle school had focused on crafting how to advocate for his learning. Then, by high school, he merely had to focus on refining these skills.

Too often I find people advocating for children with disabilities. Instead, I believe that our ultimate goal in special education is to move away from thinking of advocacy as someone acting or interceding on behalf of another, to thinking of it as students supporting or speaking in favor of something they need for themselves. Armed with a voice and tools of advocacy, students need to move from simply being consumers of what education dictates, to being leaders in their own education.

Giving and Receiving Help

Most students with disabilities have the same human desires as everyone else (e.g., help others, be loved, feel good about themselves). They want to give back to others just as much, if not more, than they want to be helped. This need for students to protect their self-esteem is especially critical during the adolescent years. In strong inclusive settings, appropriate structures are created for secondary students to receive help and at the same time help others.

To consider this particular issue, start by making a list of all of the services that are available to help students with disabilities. Exhibit 2.3 is an example of such a list that might be created in a traditional secondary school.

Exhibit 2.3 ~ Potential Supports for Students with Disabilities

1. After school tutoring
2. Resource or self-contained settings
3. Modified assignments
4. Computer technology
5. Peer supports
6. Co-teachers
7. Various other types of supports such as guidance counselors, psychologists, software, etc.

Other _____

Next make a list of all of the opportunities that are available for students with disabilities to help others.

Was this second list more difficult to complete or shorter than the first? Did it include activities/ideas such as students with disabilities serving as peer tutors in their areas of strength, serving as cross-age tutors, working in various leadership roles and clubs, doing service learning activities in the community, being involved in various after school activities or sports?

Many people are very surprised when students with disabilities are no longer motivated or seem to have developed *learned-helplessness* by the time they reach the upper grade levels. Let's consider an analogy. What if for the last five years an administrator said that your teaching was not good enough, and she always placed another teacher in your class to help. Add to this scenario that this other person was a very strong teacher who often took over for you, even at times when you were quite capable of doing the work on your own. If this happened year after year, and no one provided you with opportunities to fly on your own or, even more importantly, to share your amazing talents with others, then learned helplessness would set in for you, too.

Peer Support Structures

Earlier in the chapter, it was noted that strong inclusive schools do not diminish the traditional reward structure, but promote additional activities that allow students with disabilities to receive recognition and contribute to the learning of others. The most common approaches I have seen used are evidence-based practices that provide peer support structures, such as true peer tutoring and/ or cooperative learning. Both of these practical examples can impact students' self-esteem and enhance their learning.

Peer mentoring programs, including peer tutoring, have succeeded in boosting academic skills as well as self-esteem for many secondary students. Schools that elect to use peer tutoring should become familiar with the range of tutoring options (see Exhibit 2.4) that can be used to allow students to give and receive support (Jenkins & Jenkins, 1987).

Exhibit 2.4 ~ Types of Peer Tutoring

- **Cross Age:** an older student (could be a student with a disability) provides support to a younger student.
- **Same Age:** student tutors another student of the same age in various skill areas to ensure mastery.
- **Class-wide Peer Tutoring:** entire class of students is involved in tutor and tutee roles (Greenwood, Delquadri, & Hall, 1989).

Some basic steps that can be used when beginning a peer tutoring program are presented in Exhibit 2.5.

> **Exhibit 2.5 ~ Steps for Implementing Peer Tutoring Programs**
>
> - Select objective
> - Select and match students
> - Prepare materials
> - Determine schedule and select meeting location
> - Prepare tutors
> - Monitor program through evaluation

Chapter 5 provides more specific and creative ways to use peer mentoring models.

Cooperative Environments

Let's consider a typical lesson on the life cycle of plants. Traditionally, students might read a chapter, hear a lecture from the teacher, answer questions at the end of the chapter, and then take a test. This type of instruction may work for some in the class; however, if a student has an auditory, visual, or reading disability, then learning may be limited, not because the student is incapable of learning but because the presentation is targeted at that student's area of weakness.

Alternatively, cooperative learning is an ideal tool to address a range of students' needs in an inclusive classroom. Using structures such as "think-pair-share" or Literature Circles (Daniels, 2002) school-wide, classrooms are created in which students' strengths can be reflected. When implemented with true interdependence and accountability, a cooperative learning model allows students with disabilities to be given roles (e.g., illustrator or connector in literature) that celebrate their gifts, and do not reflect their weaknesses. Incorporating this type of approach school-wide encourages all students to become more effective at working in groups, focusing on social skills, and at the same time enables students with disabilities to contribute to their learning environments.

Service Learning

The practice of service learning provides all students, including those with disabilities, varied opportunities to give of themselves to others and to the community. By combining the areas of learning with service, these activities are curricular in nature and thus promote and reinforce the acquisition of knowledge based upon standards. For example, instead of having a project that is solely volunteer or community service (the value of which is not being minimized), service learning extends and expands on such a project by looking at the factors that surround and affect it. Thus, if students are involved in an environmental activity, they are not satisfied with merely responding to the specific need. Additionally, they are responsible for learning why the situation occurred and what can be done to eliminate or lessen it in the future. Similarly, if a service learning project includes helping children or adults learn to read, the learning component could explore the reasons for illiteracy and possible solutions to this problem. For students with disabilities, service learning is particularly appropriate as it allows them to reap the benefits of giving to their community while simultaneously developing academic skills.

Grading

Recognition and celebration of achievement and student learning cannot be fully addressed without including the topic of grading and assessment, which will be discussed at greater length in Chapter 7. At the present time, no clear-cut solutions exist to the sundry and difficult issues surrounding grading. Thus, I can only provide suggestions from inclusive schools across the country. What is clearly evident is that our educational system must devise a new and improved model of grading and assessment that honors and respects the differences of all learners, and the varied ways that learning can be demonstrated.

Adopting a system that embraces a wider range of learners and learning styles does not just benefit students with disabilities, but is helpful to all students. Remember, the theme in the book so far is consistency. In subsequent chapters, this theme continues and is expanded upon by focusing on the creation of interdisciplinary teams that are empowered to tackle the numerous concepts presented such as creating positive environments, students giving and receiving help, and the complex issue of grading.

Reflective Questions

1. How do we celebrate all students in our school?
2. What tools or activities could be added to our school to allow students with disabilities to help others?
3. How is grading addressed, and how can we use grading and assessment to expand the celebratory nature of our school and/or classroom?

References

Daniels, H. (2002). *Expository text in literature circles*. Voices from the Middle, 9(4). 7-14.

Greenwood, C. R., Delquardi, J.C., & Hall, R.V. (1989). Longitudinal effects of classwide peer tutoring. *Journal of Educational Psychology,* 81, 371-383.

Jenkins, J.R., & Jenkins, L.M. (1987). Making peer tutoring work. Educational Leadership, 44(6), 64–68. Johnson, D. W., & Johnson, R. T. (1999). *Learning together and alone: Cooperative, competitive, and individualistic learning* (5th ed.). Boston: Allyn and Bacon.

Stanton, Timothy, K. S. Giles, D.E. Cruz, N.I. *Service Learning.* 1999, Jossey-Bass, San Francisco, CA.

Chapter 3

Developing Interdisciplinary Collaboration

Most everyone in education agrees that the need for all students to be successful at reading, writing, and math is greater today than ever, due in large measure to the high stakes testing. In most cases, these tests govern both grade level promotion and, ultimately, graduation. Although testing varies from state to state, as does reporting of test scores, the outcomes of these tests have become the bottom line for many schools. In many states, both the funding and the status of schools are dependent on narrowly defined scores on a state test. This funding structure puts extreme pressure on educators and encourages teachers to focus their instruction on skills that will help students meet the testing standards. However, it is still unclear whether students' learning has increased with this stronger focus on standardized testing.

In this era of high stakes testing, the impact is particularly great for students with disabilities. Their need for more and improved instruction in the areas being evaluated is critical. Since these students were often not included in the general education curriculum during their elementary years, this push at the middle and high school levels to suddenly meet all state standards requires a miracle on the part of both students and teachers. A significant benefit of this work on behalf of students with disabilities is, that by addressing their specific needs and providing strategies for students in special education, the entire spectrum of children is better served and the richness of our diverse classrooms is more fully acknowledged. While the issues of high stakes testing are contentious, they are, for better or worse, the reality in education today. Therefore, the remaining chapters of this book focus on some practical solutions to the issues facing state departments, administrators, teachers, parents and, most importantly, students.

In strong inclusive schools, teachers cannot teach in isolation. In these schools, math relates to English, which relates to art, which relates to science, which also relates to music. This model of instruction requires a clearly defined and articulated curriculum that must be aligned to the standards. Teachers must be able to collaborate on both horizontal and vertical levels, so that concepts and skills scaffold not only from class to class but also from grade level to grade level. This interdependency can be illusive but there are tremendous rewards when it is attained. Teachers embrace the concept, "together we are better," in all that they do, including instruction of students.

Implementing this interdisciplinary model may be more easily realized in an elementary school where a single teacher provides the curriculum, but it is much more complicated and complex at the secondary level. Delivering instruction through an interdisciplinary model can be difficult in a traditional middle school but may be more successful in a *true middle school model* where teachers work as teams. However, some middle school level teams exclude elective teachers, or the special educators act as their own team. When this occurs, the result is usually disjointed instruction and learning.

In high schools, unless a model of learning communities (for more information on learning communities go to www.topschools. com) has been embraced, teachers typically work in content area teams. These teams promote high level competency in their particular content area, but cause disjointed learning related to other subject areas. Implementing more seamless delivery of instruction is beneficial for all students, but is critical (life or death) for many students with disabilities who need repetition in learning, have difficulty transitioning from one topic to the next, or have trouble tying unrelated concepts together.

The need for an interdisciplinary approach is made even more evident by recent research in the area of brain-based learning. This research shows that material is encoded more effectively when learners are given some type of visual image, musical lyric, or chant to help them retain the information. This suggests that teaching is more effective when students' brains are engaged beyond just auditory or visual encoding of letters or words. For example, think for a minute about the song, "Row, Row, Row your boat…," learned in first grade. This song, once learned, is encoded into memory and can still be recalled many years later. Now think of other word-related lessons such as the plant cycle or the phases of a cell. When these lessons are set to music, or if students are provided with stimulating ways of remembering the tasks, recall improves. However, if these lessons are taught through traditional lecture, sometimes known as drill and kill, they are less likely to be permanently engrained in memory. Is it because this song is more important than the plant cycle, or is it that it was taught in a way the brain not only learns the information but also encodes it for a lifetime?

Schools that are not merely surviving in this time of high-stakes testing but rather are actually thriving understand that learning beyond the primary senses of sight and sound is critical. In these schools the art teachers and physical education teachers are just as committed to teaching core vocabulary words as are the English teachers. This type of interdisciplinary instruction is good for all students, but is essential for students with disabilities who often learn best through modalities beyond simple lecture. However, the use of these additional modalities or avenues of learning are limited or even eliminated in many of today's secondary schools.

When teaching teams are content-specific (e.g., the science team plans together with other science teachers or the math team plans isolated from other content area staff), the instruction that follows may be rich in that particular content area but has little if any relevance beyond the confines of that specific classroom. Look at this in a real-life example: Isn't it interesting that the same students who cannot master basic content taught in isolation seem able to remember and talk about numerous details of a two to three hour movie they watched as long as five years ago? Might it be that the first fifty minutes of the movie flowed into the next fifty minutes and so forth? On the other hand, think about a movie you began to watch but just could not stay focused on. Perhaps the storyline constantly changed or there was no sense in how things were connected. The movie probably got boring. In this case, it is likely you either stopped watching or began thinking about something else.

This latter type of movie experience is similar to what many students deal with daily in secondary schools as they are currently structured. They close their math book and move to science where a new topic is introduced that has nothing to do with what they previously learned. Then they move to an elective such as art where they may again be engaged but their learning is disconnected from the previous two periods. This phenomena occurs day in and day out, and then the students are told they are having difficulty and failing. Where might the true problem lie? Have we created a situation, much like the movie, where there are few if any connections and, as a result, students are not engaged so they tune out? Thus, the question, "Is high school more difficult for students with disabilities because of the students themselves or because of the structure of the school? Does the school's disjointed structure make learning disabilities even more apparent?"

Think about a world in which everything we as adults did had nothing to do with the next thing; how long would we continue to work in such an environment? And yet we are surprised at the national dropout rate of students with disabilities. Schools that embrace the diversity of their learners understand the need for both continuity and collaboration within and across the curricular areas of the school, and are not afraid to make changes to ensure student success. The good news is that in a strong inclusive school the "movie" makes sense because of a truly collaborative approach. Students see connections between classes and there is clarity in the plot and setting of what they are to learn throughout the entire school experience.

How can schools maximize the strengths of their staff on behalf of all students? What can be done to make teaching more collaborative? One successful strategy involves empowering teams to make changes, such as:

- incorporating core vocabulary into all classes (e.g., students in music are to create lyrics from the core vocabulary words);
- finding units or themes to teach the state standards across classes not just in one environment;
- identifying "Power Standards" (the most critical information for students to learn);
- making sure all teachers are teaching all students these core standards;
- ensuring mentoring for new teachers on a team related to instructing a wide range of learners.

Fortunately, schools are starting to see that once is not always enough! They are realizing that students with disabilities may need to have repetition built into their day. One way to provide repetition is to have students take the same class twice for credit. The format of the class may change, or there may even be a different teacher. The second class may provide a more hands-on review of what was initially presented in the inclusive classroom. These dual classes are offered not just for students with disabilities but for all students. The bottom line is that good schools create environments in which secondary teachers can effectively work together to meet the needs of all students.

Supportive Collaboration

It's wonderful to hear a building administrator say, "We are an inclusive school that does a wonderful job of meeting the needs of students with disabilities." However, only about half of these "inclusive schools" create a truly welcoming school climate in which teachers work together and all students are successful. In the other half, mere lip service is given to the topic of inclusion. This is immediately evident when teachers close their classroom doors and work together only at staff meetings and create roadblocks to change.

In a school that emulates an inclusive philosophy, doors are open, teachers across disciplines talk to each other, laugh and share ideas as they pass in the halls, mentor new teachers, and embrace changes that positively impact student outcomes, both academic and social. Classrooms have two, three or occasionally even four adults in the room working with students. Students receive social skills instruction not only from a lesson plan but also from the models that are presented to them by the teachers and staff as they work together in the school. Instead of math teachers only talking to other math teachers, or special educators only sharing acronyms with other special education teachers, families of teachers are empowered by administration to allocate resources to ensure the success of all students in their family of learners – including students with disabilities.

The collaborative structures in inclusive schools are unique and different from those in traditional schools. Instead of reacting to changes in the laws or to mandates for testing, the pre-existing structure of an inclusive school enables staff to be responsive to these changes. Instead of adopting a new model or restructuring the school to meet some new requirement, the school has a clear structure that makes any change seem possible (including the arrival of a student with unique needs) because teachers are empowered to do just that — make changes.

For example, in April a middle school administrator said, "Next year we will be an inclusive school! I will honor the request of any teacher who wants to transfer. I also will honor any way you want to plan to include all students in the family structure I have developed." This administrator then empowered teaching teams to make individual determinations about how the students' needs would be met. There was a caveat that this had to be accomplished in the general education setting, unless the team could justify in writing the need for a more restrictive setting. What was the result? One team created a model where the general education teachers went into the special educator's classroom to teach rather than the special educator going in to teach in the general education classroom. Another team decided to include sixth grade students with disabilities in the general education classroom only half of the day, and then planned to include these students full days by no later than the middle of seventh grade (the students in this school looped or moved from one grade to the next with their teachers). A third team decided to use a more traditional model of co-teaching. Each approach was successful!

Why did this work? For one, the teachers on these teams were respected and empowered to make decisions to meet students' needs. The administrator set the bar high, with the clear expectation that *all* students would be included. An additional component for success was that over time the teams were truly flexible and could change as needed to meet a wider range of students' needs. Creating an environment where teachers and structures are consistent yet at the same time collaborative, teacher-driven, and administratively supported is critical to a flexible, responsive inclusive school.

In strong secondary schools collaborative structures are consistent, logical, efficient, and predictable from year to year (Mastropieri, Scruggs & Graetz, 2005). When times change, the structure may flex but is rarely dismantled. While changes may occur in the way students are taught or behavior is managed, the manner in which the team addresses these changes is mindful, planned, and purposeful. These schools embrace the strong structures that are characterized by interdisciplinary teams or families that include special education teachers. Veteran teachers expect to mentor new teachers, to share ideas related to successful inclusion, and to prepare mentors for their roles. Teachers in these schools understand that effective mentoring requires mentors possess expertise in teaching, knowledge of teacher development, reflective practice, and the skills associated with recognizing effective teaching or in this case teaching in an inclusive classroom, as well as skills in cognitive coaching (Ganser, 1999; White & Mason, 2001). Mentors understand that their role is emotional support, and they provide personable, open, caring, friendly, comfortable, and non-threatening support to new team members (Gibb & Welch, 1998; Whittaker, 2000).

Consistency should be a theme in strong inclusive schools, related both to team structures and mentor supports. Yet in many middle and high schools, teachers share that teams of teachers or co-teaching pairs are developed and then quickly — and perhaps even capriciously — changed because of a transition in leadership, or a suggestion of a better way to design a team. Imagine corporate America dismantling a structure each year or, worse yet, not having any type of structure to support people working together across departments. In effective business environments (e.g., companies outlined in the book *Built to Last* by Collins & Porras, 1994), structures may change but the organization's core philosophy stands the test of time. So, too, with schools — their philosophy and culture must remain focused on the needs of children. Whatever it takes to fulfill that mission is at the core of teaching day in and day out, ensuring that the climate is *Built to Last* yet flexible enough to embrace the unique and changing dynamics of all learners.

Standards and Curriculum

The issue of standards and curriculum in inclusive schools is addressed through the expectation of "best practices" from all teachers. This means that all staff must be familiar with research and practices that have demonstrable effectiveness. Using terminology that has been very much in vogue over the past six or so years, teachers must become pros at differentiating instruction. They must develop the mind-set that enables them to see and act upon the learning challenges of all students, including those students with disabilities. In fact, it may even be easier for general education teachers to respond to students with disabilities than their non-disabled peers because of the additional information available through IEPs and interaction with the special education staff.

Teachers typically address the unique curricular needs of students with disabilities in one of three ways:
1. Adaptations – Changes are made to the environment, curriculum, instruction and/or assessment practices in order for a student to be a successful learner.
2. Accommodations – Provisions are made in how a student accesses and demonstrates learning.
3. Modifications – Substantial changes are made in what a student is expected to learn and to demonstrate. These changes may be made in the instructional level, the content, or the performance criteria.

All three of these areas of change can be used if a student is on an alternative assessment. But, in contrast, if students are to meet the state standards and receive a standard diploma, then the most typical changes will be with adaptations and accommodations. For these students, a focus on Power Standards is very beneficial. These are the curricular goals that schools identify as critical for students to learn so that they can progress to the next grade level; they are also referred to as critical standards and/or essential knowledge.

The focus on Power Standards is sometimes expressed graphically through a knowledge pyramid (see Vaughn, Bos &

Schumm, 2003, for a visual image and further discussion of the planning pyramid). In this pyramid, essential knowledge and skills that all learners *must* know are at the bottom as the foundation. The middle section comprises what is *important* for learners to know, and the top portion includes what is *nice* for learners to know. In inclusive classrooms teachers make certain the *must* know standards are taught across content areas and, as needed, enrichment and remediation are provided to students with disabilities. The goal is to ensure that the *must know* is mastered by all students in the school.

If too many adaptations or modifications are made to the overall curriculum, then a student may not be able to meet the state standards required for a traditional diploma. This may be particularly true if students' programs include too many modifications to the curriculum in elementary school because, by the time these students reach secondary level, they do not have the prerequisite knowledge to be successfully included in the general education curriculum. That is why administrators and teachers in strong secondary schools realize the importance of interdisciplinary collaboration not only at the middle and high school levels, but also with teachers at the elementary level. Staff at all three levels work together to ensure that students who arrive from feeder schools are prepared for the standards expected at the next level. This is a perfect example of scaffolding as well as horizontal and vertical articulation.

Universal Design for Learning

Universal Design for Learning (UDL) is a concept that focuses on providing students with disabilities access to the general education curriculum. The basic assumption underlying UDL is that each student learns differently and needs a variety of strategies to master content. The concepts of UDL make sense for all learners. However, in strong inclusive schools, teachers understand and believe that this type of design for lessons is critical if learners with disabilities are to thrive. Tomlinson and McTighe (2006) discuss in great detail the importance of initially designing lessons that include differentiated instruction so that the needs of all students are met, and this is indeed what UDL is all about.

Mace and his colleagues (1998), as they were developing aspects of UDL, described it as a way of designing instruction that is appropriate for all learners, to the greatest extent possible. The purpose of UDL is to eliminate the need to retrofit instruction but rather, from the beginning, to design both instruction and the environment so that they can be accessed by all. This concept of UDL parallels the passage of the Americans with Disabilities Act (ADA) which requires all buildings that are new to be accessible for people with disabilities. Although items in buildings, such as ramps, were created to assist people in wheelchairs, these changes also are helpful for parents with children in strollers and the elderly who may have difficulty walking up stairs. Basically, everyone benefits from the provisions created by ADA. UDL follows this same principle and is a core component of inclusive schools. If general and special educators work together in inter-disciplinary teams to create lessons that can be accessed by students with disabilities, these same adaptations and accommo-dations can be beneficial to the entire range of diverse learners that may comprise any classroom. As stated by the Ohio State University Partnership team (2003), "Universal Design for Learn-ing does not remove academic challenges for students; it removes barriers to access."

Simply stated, universal design is just good teaching. It begins with the intial stages of instructional planning and includes three basic tenants, as seen in Exhibit 3.1.

Exhibit 3.1 ~ Tenants of Universal Design for Learning

Multiple means of representation — offering learners various ways of acquiring information and knowledge.

Multiple means of expression — providing learners alternatives for demonstrat-ing what they know.

Multiple means of engagement — tapping into learners' interests, offering appropriate challenges, and increasing motivation.

For additional information about UDL, The Center for Applied Special Technology (CAST), founded in 1984, defines Universal Design for Learning on their website www.CAST.org.

Creating lessons that are universally designed is critical. But of equal importance is an understanding by teachers of the essential role of teamwork. Teaching in isolation is not an option. Support at all levels is also necessary, from funds, to materials, to the way planning is scheduled: this must all reflect a "together we are better" philosophy.

The following characteristics are truly reflective of interdisciplinary, collaborative secondary schools:
- Administrators hold teams accountable and simultaneously empower them to make changes as needed.
- Co-teaching is supported but not mandated as a tool to meet a wider range of learners' needs.
- Curriculum and IEP development is a collaborative process.
- Lessons are created based on Power Standards, and are universally designed to meet the needs of a wide range of learners.
- Teachers observe each other and view their colleagues' opinions as an asset to their teaching.
- Teachers in-service each other and complete peer observations.
- Services are flexible, coordinated, and delivered in the general education setting, to the greatest extent possible.
- Collaboration is expected, rewarded, and, most importantly, valued.

Schools that embrace these components, and employ proven and promising practices such as UDL, understand that "together we are better," and they can truly be called inclusive schools.

Obstacles to Inclusion
The implementation of a truly inclusive model of instruction in secondary schools is fraught with a variety of challenges; it is also reinforced with bountiful rewards. In acknowledgement of this reality, the following suggestions are provided. They include ideas and strategies that educators across the country have identified in an effort to overcome the obstacles to inclusion. They can help teams embrace change in a meaningful and purposeful manner. Additionally, these ideas can assist teams in the creation of a

more interdisciplinary and accepting school climate for all students, one that fosters harmony among teachers and staff, as well as among a classroom of adolescent students. They reinforce the need to create a system that is mindful of all students and teachers, yet flexible enough to change as both staff and students change. These changes may need to occur weekly, monthly or yearly, but one thing that is evident in a strong inclusive school is that change, is inevitable. It is not change for the sake of change but for the purpose of creating a team of teachers who are empowered to ensure they can work together for the success of each student who enters their classrooms.

Ways to find time to meet/discuss issues and prepare for instruction

- Use teacher aides/assistants to free up time for planning during group or independent work.
- Eat lunch together to build relationships, so planning time can focus on classroom tasks.
- Give of your own time, especially in the first year of implementation.
- Use specialists' time (music, art) to meet.
- Meet before or after school (with or without financial support).
- Hire a floating substitute to cover classrooms daily.
- Ask the principal/supervisors to serve as a substitute.
- Combine classes for group activities so that teachers can plan as their classes work together on projects.
- Set agenda priorities for common planning time, making sure other tasks do not conflict with or override assigned time.
- Hire a permanent substitute who, when not needed to cover specific classes, can provide more time to plan.
- Have weekly or monthly round table discussions about topics such as grading and grouping, with which all teams struggle.
- Schedule one early dismissal day per month to allow concentrated planning or unit planning time.
- Provide, once a month, free periods for students to work on activities related to state standards, thus providing times that require less intense teacher support.
- Incorporate flexibility into the special education teacher's schedule to allow one day per week for planning.

- Change the structure of the school day to allot the last half hour for teacher collaboration.
- Have mini-conferences in the hallways during passing periods.
- Arrange for classrooms to be close in proximity so that travel time is decreased and incidental time can be used.
- Invite support staff (guidance counselor, psychologist, etc.) to team meetings one day each week.

Ways to plan instruction
- Use standard forms for all team meetings (e.g., co-planning tools, same agendas).
- Provide all teachers/team members with lesson plans that have adaptations already written (e.g. labels for students' papers who can't write their names).
- Provide weekly planning sheets each Thursday so the special educator has time to plan accommodations.
- Integrate curriculum across all content areas.
- Combine classes across content areas to allow for collaborative planning.
- Provide common planning time so that interdisciplinary lessons can be planned with overlapping concepts and content.
- Encourage teams to talk daily.
- Create a teacher assistance team to deal with more problematic issues.
- Focus on high expectations, not labels such as "Special Education."

Ways to schedule students and teachers for inclusion
- Be as flexible as possible.
- Schedule students with special needs first.
- Schedule team meetings as a priority.
- Group students with disabilities into one section, but choose a high achieving instead of a low achieving section.
- Use paraprofessionals to assist in covering general education settings.
- Schedule students with disabilities individually.
- Ensure teacher input into master schedule.
- Allow inclusive classes to schedule first, scheduling other classes around these.

- Change the schedule each quarter, if necessary.
- Try for coinciding planning time when possible (grade level, title teacher, special educator).
- Meet by teams everyday, even if just for five minutes before school.
- Plan an entire unit the spring before or at the beginning of the year so time during the week is more productive.
- Schedule classes with a balance of ability levels (don't group all nonreaders into one class).
- Review and change schedules as needed.
- Alternate days on which the special educator works in various rooms.
- Be flexible with student labels; use a cross-categorical teaching model.
- Enable students who might fall through the cracks to get special education support in inclusive classes.
- Use Title teacher/speech teacher to support students in co-teaching classes.
- Avoid placing students somewhere for one reason and depriving them of something else.

Ways to increase communication within the school
- Send newsletters to all teachers (daily or weekly) related to students' needs.
- Provide staff with one-half day in-service time before the start of each quarter.
- Provide weekly inclusive memos.
- Provide binders that contain work samples of students' strengths and needs.
- Schedule monthly portfolio review meetings.
- Provide a color-coded page of accommodations for each grade.
- Organize a teacher advisory board to oversee inclusion.
- Have an inclusion potluck/lunch meeting monthly.
- Designate time in staff meetings for teachers to collaborate.
- Provide assignment sheets that are used across classes to communicate the amount and type of daily homework each teacher is giving.
- Conduct monthly articulation meetings focused on students who are doing well as well as those who are struggling.
- Suggest teachers make once-weekly phone calls to each other to talk about life outside of school.

- Write progress reports as a team.
- Hire a permanent substitute teacher to provide more time to communicate.
- Provide common planning time when creating the master schedule.
- Create an inclusion guidelines/philosophy book.
- Hold voluntary teacher input meetings related to inclusion.
- Provide collaborative teachers with a flexible schedule.
- Have a mailbox system to communicate concerns, maybe in the form of e-mail or a blog.
- Have a "tip of the day" inclusion chalkboard in lounge.
- Hold monthly faculty or grade level meetings.

Ways to increase communication with parents
- Hold team/parent conferences, accommodating times to parents' availability.
- Schedule parent/teacher conferences once a month, such as office hours.
- Provide all parents with a weekly memo/newsletter that celebrates all students.
- Report accomplishments to parents as well as difficulties — a strength-based approach.
- Send home written notes daily, or ask students to write their own daily summaries that the teacher initials.
- Require teachers to make two parent contacts each week.
- Create good news notes that students can fill out and the teacher signs to send home.
- Develop a "Friday Big Stuff Sheet" that lists events and tests for the following week.
- Have open houses and ask a local business to provide food.
- Ensure parents, as well as students when appropriate, can attend IEP meetings.
- Encourage all parents to volunteer one hour a month in classrooms.
- Create a homework hotline or a website listing assignments and examples of how to do the homework.

Ways to increase communication with other staff (psychologists, administrators, superintendents, etc.)
- Hold weekly team meetings that bring all support staff together to talk about target students.

- Provide psychologist with one day a week to meet with staff across teams.
- Ensure administrative support by inviting them to attend a team meeting at least once a month.
- Ensure all support staff submit brief reports for monthly memos.
- Designate one person per team to communicate with outside team members.

Ways to modify the curriculum
- Schedule time for teachers to meet.
- Have last years' teachers meet with new teachers.
- Provide a list of possible testing adaptations.
- Use behavior journals to document concerns and identify success across teachers.
- Create a behavior plan across classroom and resource teachers.
- Share the general education curriculum and the IEP with all teachers.
- Schedule inclusion students in homeroom and study hall for re-teaching and review.
- Collaborate on all planning.
- Provide different textbooks with the same content at an easier reading level.
- Provide textbooks on tape or get material from www.bookshare.org.
- Share adapted assignments/tests.

Ways to adapt instruction
- Have students highlight their notes and text.
- Type up a copy of the classroom notes.
- Shorten assignments.
- Ask students to do comparable work at lower skill level.
- Vary questioning techniques.
- Use co- teaching to make accommodations, maybe even just one day a week.
- Have a special educator or paraprofessional read the test or provide it on tape recorder.
- Give tests in small groups.
- Change print/font size.
- Provide one step, oral directions.

- Provide books on tape.
- Keep students informed of their progress.
- Construct assignment goals for individual abilities.
- Provide project choices that allow students to use their strengths.
- Develop accommodation sheets for teachers.
- Provide a note taker.
- Allow for alternative response modes.

<u>Ways to deal with students with difficult behavior</u>
- Use a common disciplinary system for all classes, with consistency across all teachers: a Positive Behavioral Support Model.
- Focus school-wide on rewarding good behavior instead of acknowledging bad behavior.
- Bring student issues to teacher assistance teams for additional support.
- Hire an itinerant teacher to support students with behavior disorders across teachers.
- Use peer mediators.
- Provide a time-out area/cooling off spot that is not punitive, and that students can choose to use as needed.
- Provide behavior charts to students to assist them in working on their own behavior.
- Provide support before/after class related to behavioral issues.
- Allow students to walk the halls or take a break in a positive way before they explode.
- Provide green slips/gold slips for random acts of kindness and draw for prizes each month.
- Focus on academic and behavioral issues during planning time.
- Have behavior journals that go across classrooms.
- Create a behavior plan with classroom and resource teachers.
- Involve all school personnel, parents, and the student.
- Ensure teams talk every day about students with serious behavioral concerns.
- Provide incentives for positive behavior.
- Establish a policy that all behavior problems are addressed as they occur.

Ways to prepare students for transitions
- Plan for the transition together with student and all teachers/staff.
- Communicate with present and previous teachers.
- Consult with previous teacher weekly and then taper off gradually.
- Teach students self-advocacy skills.
- Identify all resources that are available to support the transition.
- Provide a peer to help with the transition.
- Create a peer tutoring program.
- Offer home-base groups to help students develop a sense of belonging.
- Keep students informed.
- Have student visit with teaching assistant for short periods of time before the transition occurs.
- Talk about transition as a natural occurrence.
- Provide support from the social worker as needed.
- Discuss transition issues weekly throughout the spring in team meetings.

Ways to increase peer acceptance
- Expect students to be accepting.
- Handle students with disabilities in the same manner as others (don't try to protect too much).
- Talk in all classes about how everyone learns differently.
- Use peer helpers, planned and unplanned.
- Have a social skills curriculum for all students .
- Ensure that developing tolerance begins in kindergarten.
- Have a specialist on certain disabilities come in to talk with students.
- Have a disability awareness week.
- Encourage students to read about all areas of disability.
- Allow peers to be accepted through natural occurrence.
- Have all students listed together on class lists; do not separate out included students.
- Ensure the participation of all students in school-wide activities (assemblies, behavior programs, trips).
- Use general education students as classroom aides.
- Encourage all students to be in extra curricular activities.

As we reflect upon the theme of this chapter, it should be remembered that mindful changes occur in critical areas related to both the approach to, as well as to the outcomes of, inclusion. Administrators support purposeful change, yet do not dictate how change will occur. Teachers assume they will work across disciplines and collaborate on how students will be successful in the general education setting. New teachers are supported by mentors who embrace and reflect this philosophy. Overall structures are created that ensure students, faculty, administrators, staff, and families embrace the philosophy "together we are better," and that this philosophy is reflected in every component of daily instruction. Students assume they will live, work, and grow up in a diverse community where helping others while helping themselves is an expectation, and where adult interactions reflect a strong sense of community.

Reflective Questions

1. What strengths and weaknesses does our school have regarding the inclusion of students with special needs?
2. How could we increase and improve opportunities for inclusion in our school?
3. What kinds of paradigm shifts would we expect as we move toward a more inclusive learning community?

References

Center for Universal Design (1998). *History: Ronald L. Mace, FAIA, 1941-1998*. Retrieved July 05, 2006, from http://www.design.ncsu.edu/cud/about_us/usronmace.htm.

Collins, J. C. & Porras, J. I (1994). *Built to Last: Successful Habits of Visionary Companies*. Harper Collins: NY.

Ganser, T. (1999). Coach, safety net, compass, sculptor: How mentors describe mentoring. *Contemporary Education*. 70(2), 42-45.

Gibb, G. S. Welch, M. (1998). The Utah mentor teacher academy: Evaluation of a statewide mentor program. *Teacher Education and Special Education*. 21(1), 22-33.

Mastropieri, M. A., Scruggs, T. E. & Graetz, J. E. (2005). *Cognition and learning in inclusive high school chemistry classes. Advances in learning and behavioral disabilities*, 18, 107-118.

Tomlinson, C. A. & McTighe, J. (2006). *Integrating Differentiated Instruction and Understanding by Design: Connecting Content and Kids*. Alexandra, VA: ASCD.

Vaughn, S., Bos, C. S. & Schumm, J. (2003). *Teaching exceptional, diverse, and at-risk students in the general education classroom*. Allyn and Bacon: Boston, MA.

Whitaker, S. (2000). Mentorig beginning special education teachers and the relationship to attrition. *Exceptional Children*. 66(4), 546-566.

White, M. M., C. (2001). *Mentoring induction principles and guidelines*, from http://www.cec.sped.org

Chapter 4

Implementing Effective Co-Teaching

The first three chapters of this book explored school-wide issues as they relate to inclusion; the remaining chapters will emphasize structures, strategies, and techniques at the classroom level. This specific chapter emphasizes the entitlement of students with disabilities to the expertise of both the general and special education teachers. In schools where inclusion works, the skills of both teachers are celebrated and utilized daily in classroom instruction. This avoids the risk of students with disabilities being denied the curricular knowledge of the general education teacher or the adaptations that need to be made by the special education teacher.

Also discussed are the levels of planning that are needed for effective co-teaching to occur in an inclusive school. This includes focus on both the curricular as well as the IEP goals that need to be considered in the co-teaching setting. Role definition and preparation for daily planning are addressed, and tools that can be used to assist in setting up the classroom prior to the start of the semester are identified. Numerous ideas to assist in finding planning time are presented, as are ways to create various planning structures and a format for daily planning. Finally, the reader is provided with questions to consider related to evaluating co-teaching teams in a school.

At times, I blend the concepts of co-teaching and inclusion as I see these having a symbiotic relationship. An inclusive secondary school without co-teaching classrooms is not logical in my mind. At the same time, trying to co-teach in a non-inclusive environment simply makes the co-teaching process more difficult and less effective. Therefore, this chapter looks at examples from schools where co-teaching promotes both social and academic outcomes, not just for students with disabilities, but also for all students in the learning environment. These schools understand the importance of co-planning time and of empowering teams of teachers to find creative and effective ways to meet the diverse needs of the learners on their team (Murawski, 2005).

In schools that embrace co-teaching, administrators support the collaborative process and empower teachers. This does not mean that they fully understand co-teaching or would be effective co-teachers themselves, but they must at least have a basic sense of this practice and what must occur in this service delivery model. In order to help administrators with this, several urban inclusive teams with whom I have worked required administrators to co-teach at least one lesson prior to developing their plans for inclusive structures for the upcoming year. This simple activity enabled administrators to better understand what teachers need to be successful and to develop plans to ensure the continued development of teachers' skills.

In strong inclusive education where co-teaching is embraced, the general and special education teachers are comfortable with each other and with their classroom roles (Dieker, 2001). At the core of their planning for co-teaching is at least one meeting per month at which two important questions are discussed: "Is what we are doing best practice for all students?" and "Is what we are doing good for both of us?" All too often, schools set up situations where teachers are not happy about the co-teaching setting, but there is no structure for evaluation or discussion about what needs to be changed. In a strong inclusive school, such discussions are expected, supported and celebrated as teachers identify areas in need of improvement or change (Dover, 2005; McDonnell & Fister, 2001).

In these schools, all students see the roles of the teachers as equal, yet the specific needs of students with disabilities are clearly met. Too many times, special education teachers at the secondary level fear that students might realize they do not know the content as well as their colleagues. However, when I have interviewed students they are often amazed when I ask, "Does one teacher know more than another?" A typical students' response is, "Duh, they are both teachers so they both know everything."

The Art of Co-Teaching

A secondary school may have a very collaborative climate but the *rubber does not meet the road* until two teachers from different disciplines are actually in a room, with the expectation that together they will teach a wider range of learners, and "play nice." This way of collaboratively delivering services to all students, utilizing the skills and experiences of two teachers, is called co-teaching. In the literature, co-teaching is typically defined as an approach where two teachers work together to plan for, instruct and assess a heterogeneous group of learners (Bauwens, Hourcade, & Friend, 1989).

With the changes in the reauthorized IDEA '04, more and more schools at the secondary level have adopted a co-teaching model to address the issue of special educators being highly qualified in content areas. Although in spirit this sounds like a positive move, in many schools teachers have not been given adequate preparation or planning time for these relationships to be successful. In strong secondary inclusive schools, all aspects of co-teaching, from preplanning to daily planning to ongoing evaluation, are addressed to ensure teachers are not simply in the same classrooms together but that they work as a team in a joint relationship to meet the needs of students and to model strong collaborative relationships.

Strong collaborative schools provide co-teachers with time prior to the start of the semester to discuss common issues that might arise related to areas such as grading, behavior, and parent contact. In addition, teachers meet to talk about the scope of the needs of students with disabilities as well as the curricular goals that will be taught to the class from the general education teacher's perspective. Once they are clear on classroom logistics, assessments, and the broad topics that will be taught, as well as the general needs of the students with disabilities, co-teachers can focus on daily planning. Based upon listening to and observing effective co-teaching teams, I have learned that perhaps the most significant message has to do with keeping one's eye on the ball — the need to maintain constant focus on the needs of all students, and not just those of one or two individuals. Teams share that when they sit down to plan they try to avoid talking about student-specific issues or behaviors until the entire lesson has been planned. When co-teachers start their planning time talking about a specific student, before they know it planning time is over and they have not planned lessons to meet all students' needs. Therefore, the strong recommendation is for the planning process to begin with an overview of the lessons and specific adaptations that will need to be made. Discussion about student-specific issues can then take place as time permits.

Most teams approach the planning process by agreeing to use one of the five types of teaming found in the literature. Co-teaching structures facilitate the teachers' shared responsibility for the whole class while allowing for attention to individual student needs. Descriptors of the types of co-teaching are presented in Exhibit 4.1 on the next page.

These five types vary in their commitment to planning time, equality of content knowledge, and level of trust and commitment between two teachers (see http://www.specialconnections.ku.edu for additional tools and resources including videos of these five types of co-teaching).

At the secondary level, teachers need to be reminded that all five types of co-teaching are valid and valuable, as long as students' needs are being met. However, it is important to acknowledge that these five types are hierarchical in nature: as you move down from one lead, one support to team teaching, more and more planning time, equality in content knowledge, mutual trust and respect must be present. As much as I respect and enjoy team teaching myself, the challenge of working across a team of four to six content area teachers is enormous due to the number of variables in teaching styles and just basic human interactions. Again, it must be remembered that the needs of students should drive the type of model that is used. If students with more severe needs are included in the general education setting, then the flexibility of a lead-support model may need to be utilized. Last, but not least, if a teacher is in a support role and not co-planning, co-instructing (e.g., perhaps leading the social components of the class), and co-assessing, then this does not constitute co-teaching.

Exhibit 4.1 ~ Types of Co-Teaching

(Remember that in all types both teachers co-plan, co-instruct and co-assess for "true" co-teaching to occur.)

One Lead, One Support
- one teacher serves as lead teacher
- other teacher provides support to lead teacher
- little co-planning is needed but both teachers carefully plan for their individual roles

Station Teaching
- lesson content is divided between both teachers
- instruction of students is shared but each teacher has separate responsibilities
- co-planning time is limited but both teachers plan for their station independently

Parallel Teaching
- joint planning is needed to ensure consistency of instruction in the two groups
- same content is presented by each teacher to small heterogeneous groups
- each teacher delivers instruction to half the class

Alternative Teaching
- one large group, one small (may or may not include students with disabilities) before class, at the beginning of class, or at the end
- in small group, one teacher pre-teaches, reinforces or re-teaches information to students or can also be used to provide enrichment to a group of students who are ready to move forward with the content
- joint planning is essential to discuss both the logistics of the teaching as well as to ensure both teachers are clear in the lesson objectives to be accomplished by all students

Team Teaching
- instruction is shared by both teachers
- activities are coordinated into one lesson
- there is mutual trust and commitment to the content and the learners
- co-planning must occur for equal roles to emerge

Adapted from Cook & Friend, 1995

No matter what type of co-teaching is used, in strong inclusive classrooms these models focus on serving the needs of all students, not just students with disabilities. For example, in one school teachers use the alternative teaching model to meet not only the needs of students with disabilities but to also meet the needs of students who are gifted. In this school, the general education teacher takes students out of math class for gifted enrichment two days a week for twenty-minute periods while the special educator works with students across the class. Then, three days a week for twenty minutes, the special educator provides remediation for students who need it. This model, where the teachers alternate days that they work with students at different ends of the continuum works as well for these teachers as it does for the students. This model was successful because the teachers had time to think creatively about how they would meet the needs of a diverse group of learners. They were comfortable with each other's skills as professionals, recognizing how the expertise of each contributed to student learning.

In strong inclusive schools, co-teaching is expected, supported, and embraced as one of many tools teachers can use to meet students' needs. Also, co-teaching is not limited to collaboration just between general and special education teachers, but also may be very valuable and applied in an interdisciplinary manner between and among content area teachers including teachers in elective courses. Teachers working as a team are seen as the strength of the school, and students know that they will get the support they need because of the richness of this model (see www.powerof2.org for additional resources on co-teaching).

Curriculum and IEPs

In inclusive settings teachers know that students with disabilities have two curricula that they are required to learn and master: an Individualized Education Program (better known as an IEP) and the standards provided by each state's department of education. Yet teachers and administrators in inclusive secondary schools or classrooms often expect students with disabilities to magically master the general education content, but may ignore the goals and objectives outlined in the IEP. In the past, students with learning or cognitive disabilities were removed from the general education setting because they could not master the curriculum, while students with behavior problems were removed because they could not behave. All students with disabilities were given specific learning, behavioral or social objectives that their multi-disciplinary team felt they must master to ensure their success in school and life. However, when students are included, these goals and objectives are sometimes ignored. Merely placing students in the general education setting, not giving them adequate supports, and expecting them to learn the same material in the same way as everyone else, is not inclusion, and should be called what it really is: *dumping.*

For successful inclusion to occur, students cannot simply be assigned to classrooms, and teachers cannot be expected to miraculously fix problems in isolation (Titone, 2005). Classroom teachers and students both must be supported, and at the core of that support is ongoing collaboration across the general education and special education curricula (Villa, Thousand, Nevin & Liston, 2005). In order to facilitate collaboration across the general and special education settings and to encourage teachers to address both the academic and social needs of students with disabilities, I have created a co-teaching lesson plan book (Dieker, 2006). This book is uniquely designed to guide the planning process for both the general and special education teachers. More detailed information about this planner is later provided in this chapter.

Prior to starting day-to-day planning, I am suggesting the use of two forms. Exhibit 4.2 is an "Individual Student Summary" sheet that the special educator completes prior to the start of the semester. Ideally, the special education teacher would complete this form during the student's IEP meeting. It is not a legal document like an IEP, but rather is a vehicle that summarizes what is most important for a general education teacher to know. It describes what specifically needs to be done to support a student with a disability in the general education setting.

Why is this form important? Think about a typical secondary school where general education teachers potentially work with a large number of students with disabilities, which at the secondary level may be anywhere from twenty to fifty. These teachers either receive a form such as the one above, or a batch of IEPs to read, sort through, and try to decide what in that document is most important related to their content and teaching. Interpreting these formal IEP documents can be difficult even for a veteran special educator. Faced with dozens of IEPs, the general education teacher can quickly become overwhelmed and perhaps resentful toward students before even meeting them. In contrast, when teachers receive a one-page summary such as the one in Exhibit 4.2, they are presented with the most important aspects of the student's disability from day one. This form does not negate the requirement that the general education teacher have access to the IEP, but this summary ensures that on the first day of class there is at least a sketch of what the teacher needs to know.

Exhibit 4.2 ~ Individual Student Summary Sheet: Reflective of the IEP

Student Name: _____   General Education Teacher:_____

Completed by (special education teacher):_____ Date:_____

Instructional and Behavioral Areas	Adaptations/Accommodations to Consider in General Education Setting	Additional Helpful Information
Reading		
Math		
Written Communication		
Oral Communication		
Behavior		
Grading/Assessment		

This form is also especially helpful in a co-teaching relationship. Instead of listening to a special educator trying to go through all IEPs or verbally reviewing the students' specific needs, the general educator is provided with a simple form, allowing time to process the information regarding the students with disabilities. This form can also be used in weekly planning to review the critical aspects of the student's disability for upcoming lessons.

Finally, this form, or one that is similar, can be completed for any student (e.g., student on a 504 plan, an English language learner, student who is gifted but bored and perhaps not challenged). In one school, this form is actually put on a secured server for all teachers to access. The information on the form is connected to the electronic attendance roster. Since attendance requires a teacher to use a password to access the server, the document is secure. This allows even a day-to-day substitute to learn about any specific needs of students in a given class. The information on this form also helps teachers determine what accommodations a student might need. Additionally, it facilitates interdisciplinary collaboration by providing talking points related to the unique needs of students in their teams, families or classrooms.

Just as general education teachers need information on the special education students, including adaptations and accommodations, special education teachers also need information regarding the content that will be taught. Exhibit 4.3 is an example of a form to be completed by the general education teacher. It provides a thumbnail sketch of what will be covered over a designated period of time. With this information readily available, special education teachers are prepared to make the necessary modifications or adaptations to the general education curriculum.

This type of pre-planning is critical for co-teaching and blending of the general education curriculum and students' IEP needs. General education teachers, unless it is their first year of teaching, typically have a clear outline of how they will go about meeting mandated standards in their curriculum area. In contrast, special education teachers may or may not be familiar with the standards in a particular content area. Although special education teachers are strong teachers, at the secondary level, challenges exist in knowing all content areas and providing support across numerous disciplines. Therefore, rather than the general education

Exhibit 4.3 ~ General Education Summary: Reflective of General Education Curriculum/Standards

Curriculum Area: _____

Completed by:_____ Date:_____

	Big Idea	Most Difficult Concept(s)	Minimum Level of Mastery
Week 1			
Week 2			
Week 3			
Week 4			
Week 5			
Week 6			
Week 7			
Week 8			
Week 9			

teacher only handing the special educator a set of textbooks and state/local curricular guides (to which the special educator should still have access), the content teacher provides this outline. In addition to an outline of the content, the form in Exhibit 4.3 provides a way for general educators to share "minimum levels of mastery" as well as what is anticipated to be the "most difficult concept(s)" for students to master. The special educator can then determine how to address the potentially problematic concepts and create any adaptations that might be needed for students to meet this level. The "minimum level of mastery" column addresses Power Standards that need to be met weekly. These standards were discussed at greater length in Chapter 3. This column also facilitates discussion about the benefits of the least restrictive environment if a student is not meeting this minimum level. Providing general educators with a summary for each student with unique learning needs, as in Exhibit 4.2, and special educators with a summary of the content to be taught weekly, as in Exhibit 4.3, ensures a more collaborative environment and a greater chance of successfully meeting the needs of all students.

Once both teachers are clear on what students need to learn from the general education content and in what areas students with disabilities may need accommodations, they are ready to start planning collaborative lessons together (Weiner, 2003). Finding time to plan is the number one issue expressed by teachers at all levels and is especially difficult at the secondary level where special educators may work across numerous content areas. This issue is also addressed in Chapter 3 as well as later in this chapter.

Exhibit 4.4 presents a format or tool for pre-planning in a co-teaching classroom. It has been effectively used by teams of co-teachers to develop lessons plans in as little as ten minutes (Dieker, 2001). Granted, these teams were not in their first year of teaching, but they were very effective in planning lessons in the time given. If teachers can agree to the decisions they make on Part A and B of this form, then, when they are provided with planning time, lesson preparation should be more efficient. Teachers using this form can focus on discussing students' needs instead of trying to figure out individual teachers' roles. It provides a structure through which teachers can address the global issues of their classroom prior to the start of the semester as well as guidelines for daily planning discussions. The ideal situation is for teachers to participate in joint planning, but in the real world teachers may simply have to create plans using a format such as the one provided in the co-teaching lesson plan book. More about this tool will be found at the end of this chapter.

When analyzing lesson plans I typically find that teams do not include enough focus on behavioral and social skill goals.

Therefore, I recommend that either both teachers focus on these areas collaboratively or at least one teacher focuses on ensuring that behavioral and social skills goals of students are met. These needs can be determined on Part B of Exhibit 4.4.

Exhibit 4.4 ~ Ten Minute Pre-Planning Form

Prior to the start of the semester, both teachers work together to complete this form and define their individual roles and responsibilities in each area. Addressing these issues will allow for a more effective daily planning process.

Part A

Action	General Educator	Special Educator
Behavior Plan		
Grading		
State & Local Assessments		
Parental Contact		

Part B — This section can be reviewed on a weekly basis.

Action	General Educator	Special Educator
Curricular Goal		
Type of Co-teaching you plan to use		
Strategies to meet learner needs		
Academics		
Behavioral/social skills		

Another suggested strategy for the team to consider is writing a letter to parents. Too frequently parents are not aware of how instruction occurs. Rather than identifying one teacher as a general educator and the other as a special educator, I recommend simply informing parents there will be two teachers in the classroom. I also suggest that any information sent home, whether it be additional correspondence, progress reports, report cards, etc, include the names of both teachers. And both teachers' names should be on the nameplate on the classroom door! Exhibit 4.5 is a sample of a letter you might consider using to inform parents of the co-teaching setting.

Exhibit 4.5 ~ Sample Co-Teaching Letter to Parents

Dear Parent or Guardian:

We would like to share with you a new teaching arrangement that we will be using in your son/daughter's math class this year. This year there will be two teachers working with all of the students in the class. Mr. Simms and Mrs. Dieker will both be available during this hour to assist your son/daughter. We will be using a model called "co-teaching" to meet the needs of all of the students in the class. Both of us will actively plan for and teach the class, and we will share in the grading process. We want you to feel comfortable to contact either one of us about your son/daughter's performance this semester. Additionally, we encourage you to be in touch with either of us if you have any questions about this teaching arrangement. We look forward to working with you and your son/daughter.

Sincerely,
Mr. R. Simms
Mrs. L. Dieker

A critical component when initiating a co-teaching relationship is scheduling of instructional time as well as planning time. If a teacher is working across several teachers then creativity may be necessary, as well as flexibility among team members. As more time cannot be created in a given day, teachers must use any allotted time wisely and in ways that maximize student achievement and learning outcomes.

Exhibits 4.6 and 4.7 are sample schedules that might be considered for co-teaching at the secondary level. Notice that these two schedules vary, which appears to be the trend nationally. The key seems to be scheduling student needs first and then protecting common planning time if at all possible.

At the high school level there appears to be more of a focus by special educators on being part of a specific content area team or family structure. The exception to this rule is when high schools have implemented a small learning community model and special educators have become a part of these small learning communities. An example of a high school schedule is seen in Exhibit 4.6. In this schedule the special education teacher works solely in the content area of science and provides support to all students with disabilities across the six science teachers in this high school. Notice that the schedule includes a peer tutoring program and time is split in fourth period between biology and chemistry. This teacher also was very fortunate in that administration supported his need for team planning time.

Exhibit 4.6 ~ Special Education Teacher's Sample Schedule for High School

Time	Monday	Tuesday	Wednesday	Thursday	Friday
7:30-9:00	Integrated Science	Integrated Science	Integrated Science	Integrated Science	Integrated Science
9:00-10:30*	Biology/ Integrated Science	Integrated Science/Biology	Biology/ Integrated Science	Integrated Science/ Biology	Biology/ Integrated Science
10:30-1:00	Lunch/Team Planning	Lunch/Team Planning	Lunch/Team Planning	Lunch/Team Planning	Lunch/Team Planning
1:00-2:30	Chemistry**	Biology	Chemistry**	Biology	Chemistry**
2:30-3:00	Coordinate Peer Tutoring Program – Strategy Instruction	Coordinate Peer Tutoring Program – Strategy Instruction	Coordinate Peer Tutoring Program – Strategy Instruction	Coordinate Peer Tutoring Program – Strategy Instruction	Coordinate Peer Tutoring Program – Strategy Instruction

*   In second period each day this teacher was in both biology and integrated science class, but the timing rotated from day to day.

** He only had 4 students in chemistry this year so co-teaching was limited.

In middle schools, more and more special educators appear to be aligning themselves into interdisciplinary families. The schedule that follows in Exhibit 4.7 presents a special educator who works with four content teachers. These teachers agree to give the special educator time away from their classroom one day a week so she can plan with another teacher. In return, she is available during their planning time to prepare future lessons with them.

Exhibit 4.7 ~ Special Education Teacher's Sample Schedule for Middle School

Time	Monday	Tuesday	Wednesday	Thursday	Friday
8:00	Advisory with heterogeneous group of students	Advisory with heterogeneous group of students	Advisory with heterogeneous group of students	Advisory with heterogeneous group of students	Advisory with heterogeneous group of students
8:15	Strategy Instruction	Strategy Instruction	Strategy Instruction	Strategy Instruction	Strategy Instruction
9:00	Math Co-Teaching	Planning and mtg. with L.A. Co-teacher	Math Co-teaching	Math Co-teaching	Math Co-teaching
9:45	Lang. Arts Co-teaching	Lang. Arts Co-teaching	Planning and mtg. with Math Co-teacher	Lang. Arts Co-teaching	Lang. Arts Co-teaching
10:30	Planning & mtg. w/ Social Studies Co-teacher	Science Co-teaching	Science Co-teaching	Science Co-teaching	Science Co-teaching
11:15*	Support Period	Support Period	Support Period	Support Period	Support Period
11:40	Resource Study Hall Peer Tutoring	Resource Study Hall Peer Tutoring	Resource Study Hall Peer Tutoring	Resource Study Hall Peer Tutoring	Resource Study Hall Peer Tutoring
12:00	Organization and Skills for School Success	Organization and Skills for School Success	Organization and Skills for School Success	Organization and Skills for School Success	Organization and Skills for School Success
12:25	Resource Study Hall 2 Peer Tutoring	Resource Study Hall 2 Peer Tutoring	Resource Study Hall 2 Peer Tutoring	Resource Study Hall 2 Peer Tutoring	Resource Study Hall 2 Peer Tutoring
12:45	Lunch	Lunch	Lunch	Lunch	Lunch
1:30	Social Studies Co-teaching	Social Studies Co-teaching	Social Studies Co-teaching	Planning and mtg. with Science Co-teacher	Social Studies Co-teaching
2:15	Reading Co-teaching	Reading Co-teaching	Reading Co-teaching	Reading Co-teaching	Assessment of all students in reading
3:00	Dismissal Meet w/parents, students or other teachers				

* This time was used to service students across the classes and in specials or to talk to students individually as needed. The target for this support time was determined by student-specific needs. A schedule was created for this period each Friday based upon the needs of students who struggled the prior week.

Time to Plan

One of the core issues discussed at the secondary level is planning time. What we know is that the strategies used for planning time vary from school to school. What follows are more complete descriptions of some creative solutions, as well as the pros and cons of each of them. You may wish to refer back to Chapter 3, under "Obstacles to Inclusion," where there is a summary list of strategies for finding time to plan.

Using a Co-Planner

Earlier in this chapter, I introduced the *Co-Teaching Lesson Plan Book* which I authored in 2002, and just recently revised (Dieker, 2006). It provides the general education teacher and the special education teacher with a way to plan as a team, even with limited time. Using this book, the general educator fills out the left-hand side, which is a traditional weekly lesson plan format, while the special educator fills out the right-hand side, which contains information on students' academic and behavioral needs, as well as necessary accommodations for students with disabilities. This type of planning can be completed collaboratively in a room together or independently. Either way, the key ingredient for true co-teaching is having both teachers involved in some aspect of planning. Through this co-teaching lesson plan book format, both the curricular standards and the IEP goals and objectives are addressed.

A benefit of this planner is that teachers can have a predetermined method for moving this book between them (e.g. putting it in a basket that the other teacher can run by and pick up or having a student courier it from one to the other) and still have clearly identified and planned roles for both teachers. Another positive of using this type of planning tool is that it promotes ongoing documentation of the supports used to meet the needs of students with disabilities. A potential downside to its use could occur if the general educator does not prepare lessons at least a week in advance, as without this lead time it is very difficult for the co-teacher to work effectively. If the general education teacher cannot provide at least a thumbnail sketch of planning a week in advance, co-teaching in general will be more challenging and less effective.

Reciprocal Planning by Leaving Early

Leaving one class early can allow teachers time for planning and can be a very effective strategy, provided that all teachers agree to this model. For instance, instead of the special educator having a specified planning period in the day, the general educators on the team identify time that they feel that they can support students with disabilities without the assistance of the special education teacher. Another general education colleague then reciprocates by providing the same release weekly to plan with the other peer. So, instead of the special educator having third period planning, before the beginning of the semester the team decides that the special educator will leave the social studies teacher's classroom every Wednesday to plan with science and come to science 30 minutes late every Friday to plan with the social studies teacher. This model is not perfect, but is a way to get some level of planning. Teams who have used this model share that it is more effective than not having any planning time or having a planning time that is not available for the special educator to work across teachers in the team.

However, this strategy should be used with caution. Currently, a trend exists that is jeopardizing the co-teaching model. It occurs more often at the secondary level and occurs when the special educator is used as a substitute, because it seems easy to pull a special educator from the co-teaching setting. Certainly no one would ever dream of leaving students in a classroom without any teacher! My belief is that co-teaching classrooms should be approached with the same philosophy. If the special educator or general educator (or paraprofessional) is continuously taken from the classroom, then the spirit of what is supposed to occur is hindered.

Likewise, neither co-teacher should leave the class to take care of any type of business. Just as an administrator should not ask either teacher to leave the classroom, both co-teachers must be committed to staying in the room, maximizing both of their talents to meet students' needs. Too many times the special educator functions with so many demands, including individual student behavior plans, tons of special education paperwork, and possible ongoing crises. At the same time, the general educator at the secondary level deals with mountains of grading and unbelievably high level curricular demands. Both general educators and special educators at the secondary level could use extra time in their days, but in a strong co-teaching environment both teachers focus on delivering instruction as a team and do not see classroom time as optional.

Floating Planning Period

Some special educators may choose to have a floating planning period instead of a fixed one. In this scenario, the special education teacher is with a co-teacher four out of five days a week, with one day off for planning. Similar to reciprocal planning, the specific day the special educator will not be present in this floating planning model is discussed with the team in advance to ensure everyone understands why the teacher is absent and to determine what is the best day for this to take place. This floating period allows the special educator to have planning periods across the day to plan with several co-teachers. The downside of this model is that one day a week the general education teacher is left without support from the special educator. Teams that use this model, though, indicate that it is well worth the trade off to have this collaborative planning time with each team member.

Varying Days, Varying Classrooms

Another strategy used by teachers is to vary or alternate which classes the special educator will provide support for during the week. For example, during first period, the special educator may need to serve students in two math classes. She would alternate to support one teacher on Monday and Wednesday and the other on Tuesday and Thursday. Friday is then left open to provide additional support to whichever class is most in need. This strategy can make true co-teaching more difficult and typically limits the special educator to only being able to be in a "one lead, one support" model. This type of model can be quite effective, especially in schools where there are a limited number of special education teachers (e.g. rural schools). It provides more general education teachers with support from the special education teacher, but the general education teachers must clearly understand the limitations of the special educator. Special education teachers share that they are spread so thin that they often are overwhelmed with trying to effectively support more teachers. I typically suggest that special educators try to limit their co-teaching to between four to six teachers. Yet I have seen a teacher using this model support nine teachers, making any level of planning or true co-teaching almost impossible. Special education teachers using this model should be mindful to provide clear expectations of their roles to ensure the general educator does not feel abandoned on days they are co-teaching with a teacher in another classroom.

Hire Permanent Substitutes
Some schools choose to have one or two permanent substitute teachers on staff. With this model, administrators know they have staff available to successfully support teachers. This model can also allow for rotating substitute teaching to ensure teachers have time to plan together. Furthermore, it enables the substitute teachers to know the school and the students so they can typically provide a better quality of instruction than a traditional substitute. This strategy also allows teachers to schedule specific release time during which the substitute will provide support. Teachers share that the down-side of using this model is that planning time can become sporadic if the substitute is asked to do other activities or take on different assignments.

Banking Instructional Minutes
Some schools have reduced time between clases or started school earlier to provide time for collaboration. For example, one middle school reduced passing periods by three minutes, which equaled fifteen minutes a day, and then started school ten minutes earlier, making a total of twenty five minutes daily. They banked these additional minutes of instruction and had early release for students one day every other week. As a result, teachers could meet in teams every other week on Wednesdays. The negative side of the first example is that students had less time to socialize and move between classes, potentially causing some new behavioral issues to emerge. There is also the potential of other activities being scheduled into this time, negating its use for co-planning. Another high school went even further and instead of starting at 7:30 am (which brain research tells us is an impractical time to start school for teenagers). They started classes at 10:00 am one morning a week, thus having two and a half hours per week for planning. It negated the practice of daily planning time but gave a powerful block of time once a week. As an added bonus, the teachers found that on the later start days students actually were on time for first period.

Increasing Class Size

Although this strategy may be unpopular with teachers, certain schools have found increasing class size to be most useful. One particular school added two students to each class to allow for the hiring of two fulltime substitute teachers that could be used in numerous capacities, from covering planning time to providing teaming support in some classes. Having fulltime substitutes on staff allowed for consistency when someone was away and provided some flexibility in the scheduling of classes. Of course, the benefit of this strategy is the increase in planning time, but the liability is having more students in classrooms. One school that chose this strategy shared that increased class size was not an issue because there was more in-class support, and more focused, meaningful time to plan for the needs of individual students.

Planning During a Block of Time

Some teachers suggest that lunch and planning should be scheduled back-to-back whenever possible, because in the teaming process there is need for both task and maintenance types of conversation. Maintenance conversation is critical to team development and is often referred to as small talk or pleasant conversation. This type of conversation usually focuses on talking about things such as family, haircut, weekend, and life. Task conversation focuses on preparing for a task and getting the job done. If teachers have lunch prior to planning time, the contention is that maintenance conversations will flow into task discussion, allowing more time for planning the tasks at hand. A positive aspect of this strategy is the potential development of a stronger relationship between the two teachers, as well as the provision of focused time to plan and be productive. A concern with this type of scheduling is that some teachers may want the freedom to determine how to spend their lunchtime.

Standards-Based Student-Directed Reviews

In this example, teachers set aside a block of time each week in which students work on an activity that needs minimal facilitation by the teacher, as it is generally a peer support type of review. The review is directed at the state standards and typically focuses on independent tasks students will be expected to accomplish on the state assessment. For example, each Friday a team of teachers schedules a student-directed, standards-based activity.

Basically, the students enter the classroom and are given a task, such as writing a five paragraph essay on an assigned topic that is tied to something they are studying in science or social studies. The teachers then direct the students to write a first draft of their paper on this topic (students who needed a scribe spoke their story into a video camera or tape recorder, and then students who finished early could start scribing), have two peers edit their paper, and then to write a final draft. While students initially struggled with these student-directed activities, after some coaching these teachers found that in a fifty-minute block they could find about thirty minutes to do some planning for the next week. Because they had already agreed that they would alternate in creating a student-directed activity for Fridays, they only had four days of planning to complete together.

The team in the above example chose this strategy for two reasons: First, their administrator did not initially support planning time, but they felt they could sell this model if they showed how it tied to raising students' scores on state assessments, and it gave the team more time to plan, second, these teachers were constantly helping the students, but when it came time for students to take the state assessment without their teacher's assistance, they were unprepared. This student-based, student-directed strategy helped the students become more independent in their learning and in their ability to demonstrate that learning. An added bonus was that teachers were provided with an opportunity to incorporate curricula from other subjects, providing a more interdisciplinary approach. The challenge of this model is obvious: The curriculum is already packed with so many essential standards that the teachers had to plan very strategically to ensure effectiveness. In addition, there were days when students did not behave or work as expected which meant that the planning time had to be aborted. In such cases, planning had to take place after school. The reason this worked so well for this team of teachers is that they had agreed on how they would handle the activity in advance and had a fall-back plan. When the student-directed activity did not go as expected, this fall-back plan increased the likelihood of having quality planning time.

Beyond Planning

As planning progresses and co-teaching is instituted, teams need to consider how they will evaluate this process. I recommend that prior to the start of the semester, the questions that follow be addressed by the co-teaching team. This promises to minimize (note, I did not say "avoid") ambiguity and help facilitate a successful co-teaching relationship. Too often schools implement a program and decide it does not work without employing a process of ongoing evaluation. Essential to such an evaluation process is the proactive involvement of administration. As mentioned in earlier chapters, in the quest for a truly inclusive environment, teachers can be led by administration, or teachers can take the lead themselves with the support of administration. Either way, at a minimum it is critical that administrators are aware of the co-teaching models being used, and are supportive of the need for planning. Furthermore, I encourage administrators to meet with teachers prior to starting the co-teaching process, and, no less than once a semester, they should visit classrooms and talk with teams about what is working and what can be changed to make co-teaching and inclusion successful.

1. How will we determine the success of the relationship (student grades, personal perceptions, student/parent comments)?
2. How often will we evaluate the co-teaching relationship and our effectiveness in meeting the needs of our students? WRITE DATE ON YOUR CALENDAR
3. How will we conduct this self-evaluation (talk in person, send written notes)?
4. How will we determine the students' perceptions of our co-teaching (informal evaluation, interviews)? How often will we do this? (I recommend at least once a semester) WRITE DATE ON CALENDAR
5. How will we keep our administrator involved in the process and assist him/her in evaluating progress (written notes, informal observation, team meeting)?
6. How often will we involve our administrator? (I recommend at least twice a semester.) SET UP DATE AND WRITE ON CALENDAR WITH ADMINISTRATOR
7. How and when will we involve parents in all aspects of the co-teaching relationship including the evaluation (letter home, informal phone conversations, parent meetings)? WRITE DATE ON CALENDAR
8. Finally, and most importantly, what will we do if a problem arises?

When all is said and done, co-teaching is a form of collaboration that must be embraced, supported and nurtured for the relationship to thrive. As mentioned earlier in this chapter, in a perfect world, all teachers would want to work together and there would be adequate paid time for fostering the co-teaching relationship and the co-planning that is necessary for this to occur. In the real world of a strong inclusive school there will be collaborative structures in place to facilitate working together. Even with these structures in place, however, all teams go through the development process of storming, norming, and performing. But, in inclusive schools there is a calm after the storm because teachers never veer from the main focus of successfully meeting the needs of all students in the general education setting. The calm after the storm is more difficult to achieve at the secondary level where potential roadblocks are not only the students' skills, but also the desire of adults to protect their territory. However, there is tremendous support in truly inclusive schools, as teachers expect to work together and students embrace these collaborative environments of support.

Reflective Questions

1. What conversations need to take place in our school between general and special educators to facilitate the co-teaching model?
2. How will we, as co-teachers, find time to plan, and how will we ensure that we are using our planning time effectively?
3. If our school is currently following an inclusion model, what challenges are we facing? If we have not yet begun with this model of inclusion, what can we do to make the initial steps smoother?

References

Bauwens, J., & Hourcade, J. J., & Friend, M. (1989). Cooperative teaching: A model for general and special education integration. *Remedial and Special Education, 10*, 17-22.

Cook, L. and Friend, M. (1995). Co-teaching: Guidelines for creating effective practices. *Teaching Exceptional Children, 28*, 1-16.

Dieker, L. A. (2006). *The CoTeaching Lesson Plan Book* (3rd Edition). Whitefish Bay, WI: Knowledge by Design.

Dieker, L. A. (2001). What are the characteristics of "effective" middle and high school co-taught teams for students with disabilities? *Preventing School Failure, 46*(1), 14-23.

Dover, W. F. (2005). 20 ways to consult and support students with special needs in inclusive classrooms. *Intervention in School and Clinic, 41*(1), 32-35.

Friend, M., & Reising, M. (1993). Co-teaching: An overview of the past, a glimpse at the present, and considerations for the future. *Preventing School Failure, 37*(4), 6.

McDonnell, J., & Fister, S. (2001). Supporting the inclusion of students with moderate and severe disabilities in junior high school education classes: The effects of classwide peer tutoring, multi-element curriculum, and accommodations. *Education and Treatment of Children, 24*(2), 141-160.

Murawski, M. W. (2005). Addressing diverse needs through co-teaching. *Kappa Delta Pi Record, 41*(2), 77-82.

Titone, C. (2005). The philosophy of inclusion: Roadblocks and remedies for the teacher and the teacher educator. *Journal of Educational Thought, 39*(1), 7-32.

Villa, R. A., Thousand, J. S., Nevin, A., & Liston, A. (2005). Successful inclusive practices in middle and secondary schools. *American Secondary Education, 33*(3), 33-50.

Weiner, H. M. (2003). Effective inclusion: Professional development in the context of the classroom. *Teaching Exceptional Children, 35*(6), 12-18.

Chapter 5
Establishing Active Learning Environements

Reflect for a moment on any job in society, including teaching. Consider how each of these jobs requires more than just knowledge of math, science, social studies or other content areas, but also requires essential social skills for getting along with others. For example, to be excellent and really successful at their jobs, teachers must know content, but must also be able to get along with the support staff, other teachers, administrators, students, and students' families. When we truly analyze what is needed for success in our current society, much of it is social in nature. As mentioned previously, many students with disabilities lack social skills or essential job knowledge. However, schools keep these same students isolated or fail to use tools in the general education setting that engage students and allow them to interact socially and work together, which they will be expected to do in the work force. This chapter focuses on how to cultivate essential social skills in an inclusive environment while maintaining high academic standards.

Cooperative Learning

Cooperative learning is a proven practice for impacting all students' learning (Johnson & Johnson, 1999), and along with various forms of peer support may be accurately viewed as a highly effective method for laying the groundwork for inclusion. Additionally, true cooperative learning has clearly been found to be an evidence-based practice that impacts the achievement of students with disabilities (McMaster & Fuchs, 2002). Why do I use the term "true" cooperative learning? Because many teachers have shared that they have tried cooperative learning and found it does not work. Yet upon further investigation, it becomes evident that these teachers had put kids into groups but the structures required to constitute cooperative learning did not exist.

How can educators create classroom learning environments that reflect the skills needed for the future workforce while allowing enough structure for adolescents to safely interact, and simultaneously embracing the diversity of students with disabilities in the general education setting? The answer is actually very simple—through the use of *true* cooperative learning. The traditional classroom structure in American schools involves students working quietly and independently, often at desks arranged in rows (Good & Brophy, 1987; Johnson & Johnson, 1999). Such isolation among students creates a challenge when trying to further the academic and social skills of students in inclusive settings (Pearl, 2004).

Utilizing the true components of cooperative learning (see Johnson & Johnson, 1999) counteracts this type of isolation and provides a natural structure for student interaction and social skill development. This type of interaction can be more productive than standard, individualistic efforts. The five basic elements of true cooperative learning that foster successful academic and social engagement are seen in Exhibit 5.1.

Exhibit 5.1 ~ Elements of Cooperative Learning

- Positive Interdependence: Students see the importance of working as a team and realize that they are responsible for contributing to the group's effort.
- Face-to-Face Interaction: Students work in situations that promote eye contact and social exchanges, thus allowing maximum engagement in discussions.
- Individual Accountability: Suggests that each person is responsible to the group and must be a contributing member.
- Group Behaviors: Refers to the interpersonal, social, and collaborative skills needed to work with others successfully.
- Group Processing: A time after the cooperative learning task is finished when team members reflect on their personal behavior during the process, and that of their group, with the goal of improving the group's future effectiveness.

Using these elements of cooperative learning, the following example demonstrates how a range of learners might be addressed using cooperative learning. First, the teacher decides to assign roles to the students rather than using a traditional lecture format. Then, one student is assigned the role of drawing a picture of the plant cycle, while another student is to write a two-paragraph summary from the textbook. A third student is to write five quiz questions for the group, and another student is to act out how the group thinks a plant might feel as it goes through the cycle. Finally, the fifth student in the group is to prepare a verbal report of one to two minutes to share the group's outcomes. In this type of example, a student who cannot read can draw, a student who cannot draw can provide a verbal report.

This model not only promotes group interaction, but also provides a way to value the diverse nature of learners in the classroom. Instead of a style that is based upon how the teacher learns or how the teacher was taught, this approach addresses the needs of a new era of learners whose worlds are filled with visual images and opportunities to work together in all aspects of life. At times in our secondary classrooms, this new era is lost. Through cooperative learning, many of the social skills that secondary level students need to develop can also be addressed. In this type of instruction, teachers who are worried about a student's behavior can address the issue by adding a grading component focused on behavior. A tool such as the one provided in Exhibit 5.2 could be

Exhibit 5.2 ~ Cooperative Learning Rating Form for Student Use

Peer's Name	Cooperative Role	Rate their contribution to your learning				
		1 Very little	2	3	4	5 A lot
		1 Very little	2	3	4	5 A lot
		1 Very little	2	3	4	5 A lot
		1 Very little	2	3	4	5 A lot
		1 Very little	2	3	4	5 A lot

used to measure both learning and behavioral skills. Students complete this form at the end of the activity and submit their rating of their peers' contributions to the group's learning. This form can be used by the teacher to identify students who are not being active members in their group or to conference with students who are causing conflict, and respond in an appropriate way, such as assigning a different role, or adding more structure to the group process.

Numerous examples of cooperative learning are present in the literature; Exhibit 5.3 presents the cooperative learning structures most commonly used in inclusive schools (Johnson & Johnson, 1994).

Exhibit 5.3 ~ Cooperative Learning Structures

— **Jigsaw method:** each student becomes an expert in a certain content area and teaches the other students what he/she knows;
— **Group Project:** students work together, combining their knowledge to create a project or complete an assignment;
— **Competitive Teams:** students are grouped into teams that compete against one another to demonstrate learning;
  • Student Teams-Achievement Divisions (STAD)
  • Teams-Games-Tournaments (TGT)
— **Team-Accelerated Instruction** (TAI): students are first tested to determine their skill levels and are then assigned materials appropriate to their individual skill level. Group members at the same level support each other in completing the material.

The use of cooperative learning clearly relates to the discussion of Universal Design for Learning. The natural peer support structures built into a class that uses cooperative learning provides an effective way of meeting the needs of a wide range of learners and learning needs (Pisha & Coyne, 2001). According to the National Council of Teachers of Mathematics (NCTM, 1991), learning environments should promote active learning and teaching, classroom discourse, and individual, small-group, and whole-group learning.

Cooperative Learning In Action

There are several advantages to using cooperative learning in inclusive classrooms. Cooperative learning activities can supplement or even enrich textbook readings or lectures by providing students with opportunities to practice new concepts, and also facilitate social interactions. In a cooperative discussion, students typically make connections between concrete and abstract levels of instructions. Related to social growth, cooperative learning promotes peer-to-peer discourse and oral language development skills that are often left out of curricular goals in content areas. These are skills that may be critical for students with varying disabilities.

Consider the following scenario: a math class includes six students with a range of disabilities, along with twenty-four general education students. The Individualized Education Programs (IEPs) of the students with disabilities reflect the need to improve skills ranging from basic math to social skills, behavioral goals, and oral as well as written language. If a team of teachers working to include these students into the general education setting were to look only at the general education curriculum, they would miss the opportunity to address the students' stated needs. Yet if they were to look only at the students' IEPs, they might fail to provide the general education students with sufficient instruction on the mandated academic curriculum.

In strong inclusive classrooms, lessons are universally designed to incorporate the state standards as well as address the stated needs of students with disabilities. Due to the range of skills that need to be taught, cooperative learning provides the best structure to address the spectrum of learning and behavioral needs. Students can work on group behaviors and interactions such as listening, sharing, taking turns, asking questions, using self-control, compromising, and contributing ideas, while individual tasks can also be assigned. For example, a student working on basic skills might be asked to use the calculator to check answers to problems while two other students show their peers how to work the problem. The fourth student in the group might be assigned to copy the final problem and record the steps for submission to the teacher. This type of clear individual accountability capitalizes on individual students' strengths and allows them to practice skills that may need improvement. Students approach group work with a feeling that they must engage and a belief that they have something positive to contribute.

It is critical to remember that there is a distinct and dramatic (in terms of results) difference between merely having students work in a group and having them work cooperatively. Simply placing students in groups without ensuring the true principles of cooperative learning are in place can damage self-esteem and peer relationships, or even create greater dependency. If a group of students has been assigned to do a report and only one student does all the work while the others simply watch, this is not a cooperative group. In a cooperative group, each member has a sense of individual accountability and recognizes that all students need to know the material for the group to be successful. In true cooperative learning, teachers structure the group and manage the task to ensure a cooperative relationship emerges. Simultaneously, they realize the significance of Vygostsky's words in 1962, *"What children can do together today, they can do alone tomorrow."*

Student Engagement

Just as cooperative learning can support students' increased engagement in classrooms, strong secondary inclusive schools and effective schools in general take measures to maximize engagement (see http://www.ncee.org for examples of evidence-based practices/ core principles of student engagement as defined by *America's Choice Schools*). So, why is it so important to engage students as learners? Simply stated, because learning is active, not passive. Teachers in strong inclusive schools recognize this reality and employ techniques that involve movement and active learning. They embrace laughter as a part of their teaching, and do not expect students to always be silent and sit in a row, acknowledging that this latter model is from the industrial era and is no longer needed for success in life. In a strong inclusive setting, modalities beyond listening and writing are engaged (Downing & Eichinger, 2003). Students are encouraged to work in groups and to actively engage in discussions (similar to those in the typical work place) to determine how they might better solve problems presented to them, or to learn from each other's perspectives. They are encouraged to have debates, discussions, conflicts, and even laugh as they work in a group. In reference to my own colleagues, people often come by and ask us, "What secret to happiness have you found in this suite?" We laugh all the time at work; we laugh at ourselves, and it is noteworthy to say that our suite of colleagues features some of the most productive staff at the University. Happiness, active communication, and laughter support learning and should be encouraged in the classroom. Is their absence a reason why learning is more difficult for some students? While it is important to avoid a world of chaos in the classroom, there should be a relaxed climate where learning is flexible and engaging…and fun!

Educators can promote active learning in a variety of ways. What follows are some specific tools and techniques that have been successful in helping students with disabilities have the opportunity to receive help and help others in return. When students with disabilities are provided peer support or when they are given the chance to help others (e.g., peer tutoring, service learning), then learning is definitely more active. In fact, a direct correlation exists between students giving and receiving support, and being more active in the learning process.

An example of active giving and receiving in a classroom setting is Literature Circles, which are a form of cooperative learning for reading tasks. This method allows for interdependence while at the same time enables students to participate in a meaningful way. The development of Literature Circles by Daniels (2002) focused on a constructivist process wherein students are assigned to various roles to engage them in text. Despite the strength of this process for most students in general education, many students with disabilities have difficulty with constructivist types of tasks where they are expected to learn multiple roles in the classroom (Mastropieri, Scruggs, & Sullivan, 1994). Because of this, the roles assigned to students with disabilities in an inclusive classroom are often modified, with simpler terms being given for the roles. It is also suggested that students be encouraged to master one role before being assigned to a different role in the process. To illustrate the benefits of using Literature Circles, let's think about two scenarios, and consider the level of engagement in each.

In the first scenario, a high school classroom is arranged with students seated in rows; the content being covered is *Romeo and Juliet*. The teacher asks for volunteers and this typical scene enfolds: students who are good readers and are interested in

Romeo and Juliet (not always, but many times females fit this role) volunteer to read and are completely engaged in the activity, taking turns reading out loud. Then there are students who may have decided to skip class on this specific day because they knew what was planned and expected to be bored. Still other students attend the class but are not really present, as they cannot understand the story that is being read or they do not care to understand it. In this situation, only a few students are engaged and there is no dialogue about the complex story line, except perhaps between the teacher and a few students. The engagement level is limited and clearly this is not a very strong inclusive environment.

Scenario two looks very different. Students walk into the classroom and desks are in groups of five. The teacher is using a modified form of Literature Circles. She has pre-assigned students to groups and has assigned each to one of five roles that they will complete after each five pages of the story. Typically, teachers assign roles related to students' areas of strength and skill level. The five roles in Literature Circles include the following:

Predictor — This student guesses what he thinks will happen next in the story.

Clarifier — This student leads the group and clarifies any difficult concept that the group does not understand. This student also is the only one who can ask the teacher for support in the group, so the teacher is only responding to six students instead of thirty in this class.

Questioner — This student asks one question at the end of each five pages. The student may ask a who, what, when, where or why question, and then assists the group in answering the question.

Summarizer — This student chunks what has been read in the story into ten words or less. The rest of the group counts the number of words and assists the summarizer in condensing the big idea of the last five pages into ten words or less.

Artist — This student draws throughout the class; it can be a new picture for each five-page segment, or one continuous piece of art. At the end of each five pages, this student shares the visual interpretation of the story.

The teacher in this classroom has carefully assigned roles based upon students' skills. The student who cannot read is drawing a picture. The student who is always questioning others is assigned to ask the questions. The student who needs to learn leadership skills is the clarifier. This process enhances social skill development through an appropriate secondary social skill activity that is academically engaging and enriching.

What might happen in this Literature Circle scenario is that the student who is always demanding the teacher's attention and who has been assigned to the role of the artist, asks the teacher to come over to answer a question. However, in this classroom only the clarifier can ask the teacher for help. The teacher redirects the artist to check with the clarifier (a peer) who happily addresses the student's questions, and his group then moves on to reading the text. This teacher has created a cooperative learning activity that has not only allowed students to work together and be engaged as a group, but has also reduced the number of behavioral issues and questions that need to be addressed. At the same time, the level of engagement has increased dramatically. Students are reading in small groups. They are doing their own pre- and post-reading activities and their work meets the criteria set forth for *true* cooperative learning. The students end the lesson by filling out the rating sheet provided in Exhibit 5.2 to reflect on how much they thought their peers contributed to the learning experience.

The teacher in this scenario included a way to address a wide range of learners while providing a positive forum for communication and discussions. The skills targeted in Literature Circles as well as cooperative grouping all relate to best practices in reading, learning, and inclusion. Students in the second scenario are gaining valuable skills (discourse, leadership, completing an assigned task) that are needed in today's workforce. For more on this simplified version of Literature Circles in a secondary inclusive classroom, see *Teaching Exceptional Children Plus* (Dieker & Ousley, 2006 – to download the article go to http://escholarship. bc.edu/education/tecplus/vol2/iss4/art3/). No matter what structure is used, providing students with roles for communication, engagement, and positive learning in the area of reading is especially critical at the secondary level.

To determine whether students are engaged in the learning process, consider the following questions. Doing so will help ensure that classrooms reflect effective student engagement.

1. How often are students given the chance to dialogue with a peer? How can the frequency be increased?
2. How many times during class are students given a chance to move? What are other activities that could be included to increase this number?
3. In what ways are responses elicited from more than one student in the class? How could this number be increased?
4. When do students disengage? What techniques can be used to ensure students become—and stay—move active?
5. How are students provided with a way to actively work with others on a level at which they can be successful and maintain their self-esteem?
6. How is laughter incorporated as a part of learning? How can these strategies be enhanced?

Brain Breaks

Engagement does not mean overwhelming the learner. In classrooms where learners are engaged, natural breaks in learning occur. I like to call these natural and much needed breaks "brain breaks." In engaged classrooms, a rich array of learners' needs are met through brain breaks, which are absent from the first scenario above in which the only change in the classroom was a new student reading or a teacher asking a question. A true brain break is a very simple yet critical activity that allows students to either summarize, synthesize, or to be surprised/provoked into thinking further about an idea. These breaks can be as simple as putting up a cartoon, or as complex as asking for a one-paragraph summary of the learning. These breaks should occur about every eight to ten minutes and can be facilitated by the co-teacher in a collaborative environment.

Brain research indicates that an adolescent's attention span is about eight to ten minutes (Feinstein, 2004; Jensen, 1998). For this reason, the Literature Circle example in scenario two, provides a natural brain break after every five pages. With brain breaks, learning is chunked and students do not become overwhelmed, as so often happens to secondary students with disabilities. Typically, by the end of the day, many secondary students (both those with and without disabilities) are falling apart either academically or behaviorally because they are overwhelmed and overloaded with segments of disjointed knowledge. It is important to chunk learning not only for learning's sake but, more importantly, for the protection of the learner in that environment.

Another way of promoting student engagement involves creating interdisciplinary learning experiences for students throughout the day. For instance, recent research has validated that the arts offer some of the greatest opportunities to engage students and to assist them in storing information in long-term memory (Jensen, 1998). If you have ever experienced the ride *It's a Small World* at Walt Disney World, you can see how vision, art and music can create multi-sensory experiences that are encoded to long-term memory. People leave that ride with visual images, but also with the song's lyrics in their heads, probably for the rest of their lives.

In contrast, think about the lessons learned in school. Is anything that is learned in a five-minute experience (the approximate length of the *It's a Small World* ride) stored in our memories forever? We can probably remember songs we sang or even art we created and books we read in school, but what about the facts we were asked to learn for a test? To encode information into long-term memory, the concepts should be presented in a multisensory way that embraces the arts and engages students. Strong inclusive schools value and incorporate the arts as a way to assist students in meeting the high-stakes standards they are expected to master; these are the same standards that schools are being held accountable for related to their funding. In strong inclusive schools, concepts taught in one class are interrelated to what students will be learning in various classes throughout the day.

In schools that use the recommended model of small learning communities or the middle school model, teachers plan as a team, including the special education teacher. Discussions are not about content knowledge or about standards alone, but rather are focused on students' needs and student learning across content areas. Teams and communities talk about student engagement and seamless content delivery across multiple subject areas. Students are at the core of their planning—not just students who are perceived to have the capacity to achieve, but all students, including those with disabilities.

Student-Centered Classrooms

A proverbial question of secondary educators is whether teenagers can ever be truly understood. Parents of adolescents also ask that question daily. As a teacher, I found myself at one point actually starting to believe I had figured teenagers out, at least collectively as a group. It was not until I started looking at the big picture of classrooms and schools that I realized I was actually missing the point. The purpose of education is really very simple: to teach students to learn what they need to be successful members of society. Staff, buildings, and budgets are all important but it is the students that must be the focus. Schools that are successful related to inclusive practices understand that each lesson, classroom, and building needs to be centered around learners' needs as that is why schools exist.

In strong inclusive schools, concepts such as peer tutoring, cooperative learning, and person-centered planning are embraced. Teachers work together not for their own sake, but for the sake of their students. These schools understand, as mentioned by Garner and Dietz (1996), that the person-centered approach is not about how students are served, but instead is about creating individualized and creative supports based on students' individual strengths and preferences. No longer is planning based on "the services available at the present time," which has been the age-old excuse that has restricted our thinking, planning, and actions. Instead, planning involves a team of people coming together to help develop and share in the dream of the student, ensuring the provision of supports that are necessary to make the dream become a reality.

Throughout the various stages of life, from infancy, to early childhood, to adolescence and adulthood, an individual's world is comprised of and understood in light of various spheres of influence. An infant's primary focus is getting his basic needs met; his understanding of the world is very simple and consists only of self and immediate caregivers/family members. Of course, the degree of family influence varies greatly, as does the structure of today's families. For example, only 6% of today's families fit the Norman Rockwell stereotype of a working father, stay at home mother, and two children. Yet, this is the type of family that many schools are still structured to serve (Kroth & Edge, 1997). Once a child begins school, his life is influenced by additional spheres or groups of individuals, including teachers and peers. As this occurs, the degree of influence ascribed to each group or sphere changes. Whereas parents and family are the greatest influence in a young child's life, in adolescence, amidst concerns of dating, college, and career, the influence of family often is secondary to the influence of peers. Once a child leaves school, teachers cease to be influential in the individual's life, and family may also become less influential due to physical separation.

During the entire process of growing up, the consistent center of an individual's life is himself. Teachers have only a brief role, family may become less of a presence throughout adulthood, and after school people often loose touch with peers. Teachers therefore have a responsibility to make sure that students are empowered and develop a strong sense of self. Along with academic skills, students must develop the social skills that will enable them to be successful in their interactions with others, and must understand the need of being life-long learners. Perhaps most importantly, they must become effective self-advocates, being able to understand and express their needs within the framework of adult society. Armed with this array of person-centered skills, these students are prepared to become productive members of society and are successful throughout all stages of life.

Remaining aware of the various influences in students' lives, schools that embrace the notion of students being at the center of their own lives and their own learning incorporate activities such as the ones listed below. Think about how these suggestions could impact students and how each could be incorporated into daily practice.

- Embrace the diversity of the student both from a cultural as well as a disability perspective.
- Have meaningful and ongoing contact with families.
- Provide students with disabilities the same guidance counselor access as their non-disabled peers.
- Adapt instruction to match student needs.
- Talk with students about their needs.
- Provide self-advocacy training for students and their families.
- Provide instruction that motivates and preserves self-esteem.
- Decrease competitive structures and increase individual accountability and success.

- Provide more positive reinforcement than negative (praise in public, punish in private).
- Expect students to reach their goals and maximum potential.
- Provide mentoring with local business or organizations that relate to a student's future dreams and desires.
- Allow choices in all that is taught.
- Embrace student's interests and future goals while aligning them with state standards.
- Be nurturing and affirming, yet expect the most from students.
- Use bibliotherapy, which focuses on using books to help students adjust to their disabilities (see http://www.indiana.edu/~reading/ieo/bibs/biblsec.html for a list of resources on this technique). Appendix A of this book is a compilation of books related to people with disabilities, and is printed with permission of Juanita Williams, the teacher who developed it.
- Present/provide biographies of successful people who had disabilities (e.g., the movie *Warm Springs* depicting President Roosevelt's physical disabilities.)
- Collaborate and dream with the student's family as they are the true authority on their child and have the greatest investment in and connection to that child once he or she leaves school.

How do teachers create student-centered inclusive classrooms and provide instruction that incorporates a wide range of learners at the secondary level? Exhibit 5.4 provides an overview of some of the typical tasks seen in secondary education settings (first column), followed by ways in which these tasks might be accommodated in the general education setting by the special or general education teacher. For example, if a teacher uses lecture (which is actually the least active and most difficult method for all students to learn) as the primary vehicle for teaching, this Exhibit provides ways to modify the lesson, taking into account the various disabilities that might exist in the general education setting.

Exhibit 5.4 ~ Modifications from Traditional to Inclusive Instruction

Traditional Task →	*VISUAL SUPPORTS*	Auditory Supports	**Processing Supports**	Behavioral Supports	*Alternative Approaches*
Lecturing	Display notes or images on the board.	Allow for verbal summary with peers.	Allow breaks every 5-10 minutes to review information covered.	Allow breaks for physical movement.	Allow students to talk about material in groups.
Reading aloud in class	Allow students to only listen, or use strategies that allow students to read only when they want to read in the class.	Provide students with a copy of the book to look at.	Allow students to pre-read the text.	Give leadership roles to students with behavior challenges.	Have students read in pairs using a strategy such as predictions.
Taking notes	Provide a scribe or a hard copy of notes.	Provide a copy of notes in advance.	Provide a copy of notes with only a few words missing, and have students fill in missing words.	Allow students to write notes on the board.	Provide a scribe or a copy of notes.
Writing a book report	Allow students to dictate their reports.	Ask students to provide a visual image to share with the class when presenting reports.	Provide an outline to assist with processing.	Allow students to do a team report, or ensure that material for reading is above skill level.	Allow students to choose their reading material and use an exhibition format for their final report.
Taking a test	Allow students extra time and provide someone to read the test to them.	Provide visual prompts on test.	Allow additional time or provide modified test.	Provide a forum to ask questions and an alternative location if needed.	Use nontraditional methods of assessment (e.g. exhibitions, portfolios).
Group work	Allow student to take on a role that does not require visual skills.	Set rules, such as one person talks at a time, and use a location with the least amount of noise.	Designate a peer of choice to summarize comments or clarify issues.	Provide a leadership role or assign favorite role.	Assign roles based on strengths not weaknesses.

Family collaboration

Adolescence is a difficult time, not only for students, but for everyone around them, including their teachers and families. The role of the parent during adolescence is especially challenging. Teenagers tend to want to move away from parental influence, but research indicates that when parents are involved in their children's lives, learning increases. The list that follows offers suggestions of ways to involve parents at the secondary level.

Web Resources — The World Wide Web provides a host of resources that are targeted at helping parents work effectively with their adolescent children. A small sample of helpful websites include:

- http://www.pta.org
- http://www.kn.pacbell.com
- http://www.cec.sped.org
- http://www.talkingwithkids.org

Parent Authority — Setting limits is a great parental challenge. The National Assessment of Education Progress (NAEP) suggests that parents can exert authority with teenagers. The school may think about creating a way to help families set limits in these areas:

- preventing student absenteeism,
- providing a variety of reading materials in the home, and
- eliminating excessive television watching.

Parent Role in Academics — Parents' involvement in their children's learning has a greater influence on academic success than the economic level of the family. Parent engagement is a must.

Television — Research shows that children who watch television more than ten hours per week show a decrease in academic achievement.

Routines — Students are more successful when their households have dependable routines.

Fair and Consistent Rules — Parents should set and enforce rules for their children, and it is very important for them to explain and discuss these rules as a family. Parents should also reinforce one of the primary tenants of successful inclusive schools: *Fair Is Not Always Equal* and *Everyone Gets What They Need.*

Out of School Activities — Parents should guide and monitor their child's out of school activities. Teachers may want to share a list of resources for community service activities that parents and children may discuss together.

Talk with Child — Parents should communicate regularly with their child; higher achievement and daily communication with a parent are correlated.

Talk with School — The greater consistency with which parents are informed about their child's progress by the school, the greater the impact on achievement.

Technology

How can technology be used to engage students? How can it be used to improve the educational outcomes for students with special needs? What safeguards can be used to ensure that technology is used not for its own sake but for the benefit it offers to learners?

The potential is greater than ever for technology to assist in the teaching-learning process, and most specifically to assist students with disabilities in both accessing the curriculum as well as engaging in learning. However, taking advantage of technological assistive devices is not as simple as just placing a piece of hardware in a classroom or providing software for a specific student. Technology should adapt to the changing needs of learners as they progress through the grade levels, and facilitate their ability to function in the least restrictive environment. When technology is utilized with inclusion in mind, both access and engagement are ensured. Using appropriate technology for all students, including students with special needs, promotes effective and inclusive education for all.

Technology provides tools for teachers to create universally designed instruction. In addition, technology automatically puts the student at the center of learning and allows for choices in what is learned and how it is learned, as well as how the knowledge will be assessed. Combining the use of numerous technological tools with a concept such as exhibitions (as explained in Chapter 7), provides students with multiple ways of presenting what they know. Technology used in inclusive classrooms also allows teachers to present the curriculum in different ways while providing tools to meet the wide range of learning styles.

Merely providing students access to technology is not sufficient. Students in inclusive environments need to be given permission to use these tools, and need to feel comfortable using them in front of their peers. Students with disabilities should never have to defend their use of technology tools to assist them as learners. Rather, it should be expected that students would have such tools. They must also be provided training so that they can develop skills to use the technology (e.g., keyboarding skills or ongoing instruction on how to use various software).

Even with access, acceptance, and training, students must still be engaged in learning. For students to be truly included and engaged in the general education setting they should have access to the technology and at the same time be actively involved in all academic and social aspects of the learning environment.

Some wonderful new tools are available to assist students with reading and/or writing. Two websites to consider for students who struggle as readers are Book Share (www.bookshare.org), and Project Gutenberg (www.promo.net/pg). These sites provide text in electronic format and offer numerous options for students with disabilities. Book Share, a site that can only be used by students with identified disabilities, enables people with visual or other print disabilities to share scanned books. This site is allowed to exist due to an exemption in the copyright law, which allows open use only for people with print disabilities. Project Gutenberg makes material available to the general public in electronic format. This site provides materials that are no longer copyright protected, typically due to the age of the material.

Teachers can use materials accessed from these sites to make accommodations for students with disabilities. For example, the material can be pasted into a program like Microsoft Word to enlarge print, or the text can be summarized by using a feature in Microsoft Word that is called "auto summarize," which condenses the amount of text a student is expected to read. This feature in

Microsoft Word was developed to summarize text for executives so they did not have to review as much material. With the same purpose in mind, it can be used for students who have trouble reading lengthy text. Additionally, this same electronic text can be copied and pasted into a program called Write Outloud (www.donjohnston.com). With this program, the text is read aloud by the computer to the struggling reader.

Low-tech ideas that can be used to assist students with text involve the use of items such as erasable highlighters and post-it notes. Giving post-it notes to high level readers and asking them to write one-sentence summaries on each page of text they read can be very effective. This activity improves the high level reader's summary skills while at the same time provides a ready-made accommodation for a lower functioning student in the class. An erasable highlighter and highlighter tape can be used in the same way.

Technology tools are also available to assist students with written expression. A program called Co-Writer provides students with a prediction tool that is based upon grammar pattern use. This prediction tool can assist students who have physical difficulties with typing large amounts of text, as well as students who have difficulty spelling or predicting the next word. Allowing students who have difficulties using paper and pencil to use advanced technologies may assist them in meeting daily goals and state standards.

The following checklist will help ensure that schools will be student centered and inclusive in the use of all tools related to students being successful learners:
- Administrators and teachers are committed to continued professional development for the precise purpose of improving teaching and learning for all students, including the learning of new evidence-based practices and incorporating cutting edge technology to impact engagement, access, and learning.
- All staff foster student resiliency by building on students' strengths.
- Teachers believe all students can succeed.
- Teachers provide instruction that connects with the students' lives.

- All students are academically challenged by a curriculum that develops high-level thinking skills, as well as basic skills.
- Students believe that their teachers and peers care about them as individuals, yet take responsibility for their own learning.
- Students participate in meaningful, engaged learning that relates to their lives outside of school.
- Students and teachers work together in a collaborative environment.
- Parents and community members are involved in educating students and have a voice in important school decisions, such as resources and staffing.
- Technological tools are provided to support student learning.
- Assessment tools reflect a variety of ways of learning.

Basically, for inclusion to work, teachers must teach differently or, better yet, teach to the way each student learns. This statement is a tall order in schools with twenty-five to thirty students per class, where teachers teach six different classes a day. Teaching differently does not mean that each class must be a Hollywood production. But it does mean that teachers must know their students and their interests, while ensuring all students are engaged in learning. This challenge often is greater at the secondary level, but in the amazing classrooms I have seen, teachers take on this issue by meeting the needs of each student, by engaging students, and by ensuring that laughter, self-esteem and learning are at a premium every day for all students.

Reflective Questions

1. How does our school use cooperative learning in all classes? How are the components of *true* cooperative learning used in our classroom?
2. What strategies do we currently use that engage all students? How might we improve the level of engagement of students?
3. What memory strategies could we incorporate into our classroom? What content knowledge might the music, art and physical education teachers incorporate into their classrooms?
4. How does our child study team focus on student-centered planning? What ideas might our team think of to put students more at the center of instruction in our school?
5. What type of technology is used in our school? How are students empowered to use technology to support their learning?

References

Daniels, H. (2002). *Literature circles: Voice and choice in book clubs and reading groups.* (3rd ed.). Portland, ME: Stenhouse.

Dieker, L. & Ousley, D. (2006). Speaking the Same Language: Bringing together Highly-Qualified Secondary English and Special Education Teachers. *Teaching Exceptional Children Plus,* http://escholarship.bc.edu/education/tecplus/vol2/iss4/art3.

Downing, J. & Eichinger, J. (2003). Creating learning opportunities for students with severe disabilities in inclusive classrooms. *Teaching Exceptional Children, 36(1), 26-31.*

Feinstein, S. (2004). *Secrets of the teenage brain.* San Diego, CA: The Brain Store.

Garner, H. & Dietz, L. (1996). Person-Centered Planning: Maps and Paths to the Future. *Four Runner,* 11(5). 1-2.

Good, T. L., & Brophy, J. (1987). *Looking in classrooms.* (4th ed.). New York: Harper & Row.

Jensen, E. (1998). *Teaching with the brain in mind.* Alexandria, VA: Association for Supervision and Curriculum Development.

Johnson, R. T., & Johnson, D. W. (1994). An overview of cooperative learning. In J. Thousand, A. Villa & A. Nevin (Eds.), *Creativity and collaborative learning.* Baltimore: Brookes Press.

Johnson, D. W., & Johnson, R. T. (1999). *Learning together and alone: Cooperative, competitive, and individualistic learning* (5th ed.). Boston: Allyn and Bacon.

Kroth, R. L. & Edge, D. (1997). *Strategies for communicating with parents and families of exceptional children* (3rd Ed.). Denver, CO: Love Publishing Company.

Mastropieri, Scruggs, & Sullivan (1994). Promoting Relational Thinking: Elborative Interrogatin for students with mild disabilities. *Exceptional Children*, 60, 450-457.

McMaster, K. N., & Fuchs, D. (2002). Effects of cooperative learning on the academic achievement of students with learning disabilities: An update of tateyama-sniezek's review. *Learning Disabilities Research and Practice, 17*(2), 107-117.

National Council of Teachers of Mathematics. (1991). *Professional standards for teaching mathematics.* Reston, VA: Author.

Pearl, C. E. (2004). *Implementation of co-teaching model practices and their impact on outcomes for students with learning disabilities in middle school mathematics classrooms.* Unpublished Dissertation, University of Central Florida, Orlando.

Pisha, B. & Coyne, P. (2001). From the start: The promise of universal design for leanring. *Remedial and Special Education*, 22(4), 197-203.

Vygotsky, L.S. (1962) *Thought and Language.* Cambridge, MA: MIT Press.

Chapter 6

Implementing Successful Instruction

Research and Practice

Placing students at the center of their learning and engaging them in that learning process through various means in the classroom is critical, as is using all that is known from research and best practice that facilitates reaching and teaching those students who may not have been successful in past learning environments. This chapter provides an eclectic group of practical ideas and suggestions that are based upon insights from current and emerging research into teaching of secondary students with disabilities. Considering these suggestions and then identifying those that seem applicable to a particular situation may help teachers address the tremendous challenges of educating adolescents.

From recent research using MRI's and CAT scans, much is being gleaned about what is needed for students to learn and retain new information, and about what teaching methods need to be examined. Although this research is not conclusive, the current work in the field of the brain and learning offers secondary educators some interesting concepts to consider in their practice. Also, current research identifies a number of learning differences between males and females that need to be understood. In strong inclusive classrooms where students have attention, learning, sensory, or behavioral issues, some consistent themes from recent research can impact the likelihood of student success. As mentioned in Chapter 5, when students are engaged, work together as a team, and are provided tools such as technology to allow them access to curriculum, then learning does increase. Although all of these factors are generally accepted as essential to good teaching, the bottom line is their consistent application in secondary schools and classrooms.

Some of the most interesting and pertinent trends to emerge relate to the effectiveness of incorporating repetition, movement, laughter, and the unique needs of the male and female brain into teaching practices. Added to these is the need to ensure that reading and writing are taught across the curriculum.

Repetition

Remembering information can be challenging at every stage of life, but for many students with disabilities, either long-term and/ or short-term memory impairments, are present. Current research has provided educators with some basic information about memory, but much of it is not being sufficiently incorporated in inclusive settings. For example, students must go through a process of repetition to remember information. Too often, the curriculum is crammed so full that there is insufficient time for repetition. The result is that the process of remembering information is limited. How might this be addressed in an inclusive classroom? Perhaps the general education teacher can co-plan with the special educator who is responsible for identifying engaging activities to assist students with long-term memory. Maybe the main goal or big idea to be covered in the lesson could be written into the plans not just once, but ten times, which is the number needed for automaticity and long term recall of facts (e.g., for students to remember at May testing the items that were presented the first week of school).

Great inclusive classrooms engage all parts of the brain and ask students to think about how things feel, taste, smell, sound, and look (Jensen, 1998; Sprenger, 2002). I often suggest that secondary educators make monthly visits to elementary classrooms, especially kindergartens. There, they will see little children touching, smelling, and tasting all things — even things they are not supposed to. I also challenge secondary educators to consider if the gap of knowledge is really greater in a secondary classroom than in kindergarten.

Is inclusion really easier in kindergarten, or are kindergarten classrooms more conducive to students who learn information in a variety of ways? Are students more engaged in kindergarten? Consider for a moment children coming to kindergarten who can already read sitting next to those who don't know their ABCs. And then there are the children who may not even be toilet trained or able to feed themselves. Yet many times, this wide range of skills can be accommodated in a kindergarten classroom. Is it because the gap is less than in secondary schools, or is the teaching more appropriate? The level of engagement, individualization, and multisensory instruction at this early level is something secondary educators have to ponder regularly. Yes, the curricular standards are more difficult in middle and high school. Yes, students come with huge gaps in their knowledge, but why is that? How can we move from blaming the student or the previous teacher to creating environments in which differences among students are assumed, and teaching addresses these differences?

Movement

A simple yet powerful key to the issue of student engagement is movement. Please notice I did not say chaos, but movement. The best teachers realize that teenagers need to move! I often think about this issue when I have to attend a faculty meeting or an all-day workshop. If the presenter is good, then there is usually a planned opportunity for participants to move around a bit. Yet in class, many students are expected to sit quietly and absorb information for one hundred and eighty days a year.

One of the mantras in my work related to inclusion is, if you really want to learn about your program — ask the students. In a recent day of conducting focus groups with middle school students, I asked five different groups about the amount of movement that occurred in their school. They were not sure why I was laughing as they responded, but I found their responses humorous. When I asked the five groups the question, "Is there enough movement in your school throughout the day?" the boys became angry and responded with statements, such as, "No way," or, "Prisoners get to move more than we do," or, "No one trusts us enough to let us out of our seats, but they don't get that being stuck in our seats is why we are crazy." On the other hand, about 85% of the girls responded by saying things like, "I don't want to sweat; it will mess up my makeup," or, "The boys need to move, but we don't," or, "I look too good to move." This range of comments made me think about two things. First, we test students, survey teachers, survey parents, but do we ever ask kids in our schools what they need? In great schools we do – and we especially talk to students with disabilities about their experiences, as well as talk to students without disabilities about how teaching to a range of differences impacts their learning. Secondly, groups of students may need different things (e.g., amount of movement), yet how do we know unless we ask?

Here are just a few ideas to allow safe movement, even in classes as large as thirty to thirty-five students. It is interesting to note that movement is generally a non-issue in lab classes or classes that use cooperative learning. Consider trying ideas from this list each day, or add a few other ideas to this list:

- Direct students to move in the following ways:
    — Stand up, touch your toes, and say one key word from today's lesson as you sit down.
    — Stand up, spin around twice, and share two ideas with a peer as you sit down.
    — In your seat, raise your right arm and left leg.
    — Do three neck roles, and think of the main point in the lecture.
    — Rub your head and rub your tummy in opposite directions, while naming the two science terms from the lesson.
    — Walk around the room in a circle and when the music stops, talk to the person across the circle about the lesson.
- Provide a walking zone for students who may need more movement; allow these students to walk to and from the pencil sharpener, but arrange their seats so they do not disturb others.
- Have students pass books back over their heads to peers (of course talk first about how to do this safely).
- Start a first period class (when most adolescents are still sleeping) by doing five jumping jacks.
- End class with a standing conversation about the day's lesson.
- Have a three minute "coffee club" where students can sit and chat on the floor in a group, or stand and talk, but

only about a sentence that is on the board. If they are off topic, then ask them to return to their seats. If they want to socialize, after a few days they will stay on topic — I have seen this in action.

Remember that movement is needed to keep students awake and at the same time helps students master the content being presented. Although movement does not guarantee students will attend to or understand material presented, it certainly can be another tool for helping a range of learners in a classroom.

Attention
Another argument against inclusion at the secondary level is that students lack the ability to attend to the task at hand. One might counter by asking if, at times, the students are simply bored. Even though it is impossible to get all students to attend one hundred percent of the time, great teachers will go to any lengths to engage students. However, a great level of misunderstanding about attention and learning still exists in today's classrooms.

As you are reading this paragraph I am assuming that your hand is touching something. Wherever your hand is at the moment — FREEZE. Now, until I asked your brain to consider the location of your hand, your brain had probably dismissed that as unnecessary information. From recent brain research it is known that ninety percent of all that our senses pick up is dismissed; otherwise, the brain would quickly be short-circuited with too much information (Jensen, 1998). Therefore, students who struggle to process even ten percent of what is important in a lesson must be provided with instruction that is very focused on the learning of key components. We must be very clear about what we expect students to learn.

Another misperception is that people *pay attention.* Have you ever heard a teacher say to a student, "You need to *pay attention.*" What does this really mean? Is the student motivated to engage himself in learning so that he is no longer bored with what is being taught? In strong inclusive classrooms, teachers realize that both attention and understanding are the responsibility of the teacher, not the student. I like to say, "Students are not attention deficient, but we as teachers are deficient at getting their attention." I often follow this comment with the thought that if an environment is really boring and we give a student medication for attention issues, despite the medication that may make the student sit quietly, the environment is still boring and the problem still exists. This statement is not to say that parents and students should not have the right to explore medication as a tool to help with learning. But as a society, we must realize that when a child can pay attention in all other environments except school, the problem most likely does not lie within the child. As parents of a child with Tourette Syndrome, my husband and I have explored and tried the medication option. We found that, in our case, medication only masked some issues and created new ones; it was not the answer for us. Again, parents should consider this option, however in our case medication was not advisable. The wonderful teachers in our son's life have helped him understand his responsibility as a learner, yet challenge themselves to find ways to engage a very different kind of mind in their classroom.

How does all of this relate to strong inclusive classrooms? In inclusive classrooms, goals are clear, lessons are exciting, engaging and empowering, and teachers usually talk much less than students dialogue. Noise is welcomed and classrooms are no longer created for the industrial era with rows meant for assembly-line work. Students interact with their peers in groups and think creatively, mastering some of the solid foundational skills needed to succeed, not only in school, but in life. In strong inclusive classrooms, students with disabilities often become students with abilities to be successful in school and life.

Laughter

Another characteristic of many inclusive secondary schools is laughter. Have you ever walked down the hall of a school and found all children fully engaged, including students with disabilities? Have you ever walked into a school and noticed that in every classroom children seem to be falling out of their chairs laughing? Have you ever encountered a school full of adolescents where laughing at oneself is okay? There are lots of great teachers and classrooms that have the spirit of engagement and laughter and promote strong self-esteem, but rarely do we see these principles at the core of a school's culture. Instead, we see principles such as respect for all, high standards for learning, promoting excellence for all learners. While these are noble and important principles, they may not be realistic, culturally relevant, attainable, or broad enough to create a climate that focuses on the acceptance of all learners. The principles of engagement, movement and laughter are interesting and are strongly supported by past effective teaching research and recent brain research related to what students need to retain information in their long-term memory.

Laughter is not only helpful for mastering academic concepts, but is also a great way to relieve stress. There are times we can remember a joke someone told us, yet we can't remember that person's name. We often remember something funny we saw in a movie, but may not remember much else about it. Students may be quick to share stories that make people laugh, but rarely do they stop others in the hall to share some content knowledge they learned. An interesting example of the power of laughter follows: A principal I know always ends assemblies with a good joke. Students often appear to be sleeping or passing notes, as is typical of adolescents, but when it comes time for the principal to share the joke, all the students in the auditorium seem to be on the edge of their seats awaiting the punch line. Some jokes, of course, are better hits than others; yet laughter is at the core of this school. One of the school's mantras is, "We as a staff plan to laugh at ourselves before anyone else gets a chance to laugh at us first." Although this may sound strange, what these educators have learned is that if they are willing to say things like, "Can you believe that I misspelled that word on the board in front of all of you?" or, "Can you believe I spilled my coffee all over your papers as I was grading them yesterday?" they are setting an example that not all things in life are a crisis. They also are saying that no one in the school is allowed to laugh at me unless I first laugh at myself.

Some specific techniques that can help promote laughter follow. Remember, adolescent laughter is often hard to understand; it may be easy to get started and contagious once it starts.
- Make up a funny story about four terms in geography.
- Ask students to bring in their favorite cartoons from the paper for extra credit. Just two weeks after requesting this from 150 students, one teacher had enough cartoons to last throughout the entire school year.
- Have a two minute laughing contest to see who has the funniest laugh
- Allow students to submit appropriate jokes to a joke box, and select one joke to be read each week.

- Try to find some reason every day to laugh at yourself in your teaching.
- As a brain break, ask students to laugh for thirty seconds (just be warned, it will take them another ninety seconds or more to stop).
- Ask the principal and other staff members to come by and share stories about something funny they did in life or at school.
- Have a laugh-a-thon. Ask students to have a laugh-in and challenge them to bring in appropriate items to get everyone to laugh.
- Ask students to draw a picture of themselves in an appropriate yet humorous way, using the vocabulary words from the day's lesson.
- Put a cartoon or a joke in the middle of a test to invoke laughter and relaxation during testing.
- When giving the state test, ask students to stop for ten seconds, and put up a great cartoon that will get them to laugh and relax for just a few seconds.

Schools, teachers and classrooms that encourage laughter understand the equation that laughter equals learning. Actually, recent research shows that laughter relaxes the face, chest, spine and abdominal muscles, which often are taxed from sitting upright in a desk all day. Research also indicates that laughter:
- Reduces serum cortical (a hormone released during the stress response). *Like when students are taking state tests.*
- Increases tolerance to pain. – *A given issue when working with adolescents. (HINT: You are suppose to laugh at this statement).*
- Increases heart rate, pulse rate, and "juggles" the internal organs (Sultanoff, 1995). *Which is often needed during first hour in a secondary classroom; all secondary teachers know exactly what I mean.*

In summary, as schools consider a philosophy related to inclusion, the topic of laughter should be included in the discussion. How much are students laughing and how do we create a climate where we can laugh at ourselves, but where others will not be allowed to laugh at us?

Gender and Intelligence

Another key element in a strong inclusive classroom is emotional safety. It is well known that emotion has a strong impact on how much students pay attention and that different emotions are triggered in boys and girls, especially in adolescence (Kindlon & Thompson,1999; Pipher, 1995; Pollack, 1999). In a recent issue of *Educational Leadership*, a wonderful article (Gurian & Stevens, 2004) appeared about the context of the male and female brain in classrooms. From that work, I constructed Exhibit 6.1, which provides information for strong consideration as students are included in a secondary classroom. Each point ends with a reflective question to consider in your school or classroom. Remember, too, during the first five to eight years of students' lives, the majority of male students (who make up a greater percentage of students with disabilities, especially in the area of emotional/behavioral disorders) have been taught by female teachers. Not to say that female teachers in elementary schools are not wonderful, but just to point out that many times we teach to our gender and to the way we learn. If female teachers dominate the early grades, male students may come to the secondary level frustrated, not just because they may be behind in their skills, but also due to a lack of teaching in the way they learn (see Newsweek for an issue called *The Boy Crisis)*. That is why in great classrooms both gender and multiple intelligences are embraced as teachers create learning environments with students at the center (D'Arcangelo, 1998).

Adolescent Brain

Addressing the differences between males and females is important. But an equally important issue in adolescence is addressing the growth of the areas of the brain related to pleasure (Feinstein, 2004). This growth is not surprising because of all of the changes and interests that emerge during the adolescent years – changing of the body, learning to drive, dating, the list goes on and on and on. Add to this the competing outside pleasures craved by teenagers: video games, celebrities, drugs, etc. Awareness of these issues has improved over time (e.g., more open discussions about dating, more body awareness), but have our schools really responded to this?

Exhibit 6.1 ~ Reflections on the Male and Female Brain

What follows are not absolute truths for all males and females, but are trends identified in recent brain research; they are worthy of serious consideration.

Brain Research	Males	Females
Spatial-Mechanical Relationships — moving things through space	Half the brain dedicated to this area — Are you wisely teaching to this half?	An area that has to be developed in the brain — How do you encourage females in your classroom in this direction of learning?
Verbal-Emotional Functioning — talking and feeling	Experience words and feelings differently than girls — How are opportunities provided to talk about feelings in a safe context?	Half the brain dedicated to this area — Are you wisely teaching to this half? Are times for socialization and talking about feelings included as a part of the curriculum?
Hormones	More impulsive and less likely to sit and listen or show empathy — How is movement a part of your environment?	A natural high to talk and listen with others, think before acting and more likely to show empathy due to hormonal differences — Are empathetic types of activities built into your curriculum?
Sleep and Rest	Enter a rest state more frequently and will need more breaks to ensure they do not fall asleep or stop paying attention; the more words used, the quicker the rest state occurs — How are movement and brain breaks used to assist with this area?	Renew and recharge their brains without needing to go into a rest state. Need rest state less when lesson is more verbal — How do you allow for verbal brain breaks to keep students actively engaged?
Motor Skills	Fine motor tasks are not as advanced as in girls; need more practice in this area — How do you include fine motor activities?	Large or gross motor skills are not as refined as boys; need more practice in this area — How do you allow development of gross motor skills?
Lessons	Experiential and kinesthetic learning is preferred. Keep verbal directions short — How much hands-on learning is provided in your teaching?	Groups and team are needed to promote leadership and negotiation skills — Are leadership roles in activities given to students who might be more engaged by leading?

Adapted from Gurian & Stevens, 2004

In a flurry of media exposure, Bill Gates and Oprah Winfrey have recently teamed up to look at our high schools in general. In a recent interview, Gates stated, "Until the schools are redesigned we will be limiting — even ruining — the lives of millions of Americans every year." He goes on further to mention that only one out of three graduating high school students is ready for college, work, and citizenship, and these statistics do not differentiate for students with disabilities. Recent literature on the learning process can be very helpful in the development of strategies to prevent students from becoming overwhelmed as well as meeting the challenge of ensuring that students, including those with disabilities, learn and master content. The goal is to understand the general process of learning and then move to ideas for bringing more interactions, engagement, active learning and pleasure into classrooms for all students, while maintaining a strong focus on the fragile egos and unique needs of learners with disabilities.

Learning is richer when we relate what we are trying to learn at the time (working memory) with information we have stored from the past. In strong inclusive classrooms, learning is connected to real life examples—those of the students in today's world, not those of the teacher from twenty years ago. That is why students being active and talking with their peers is a critical part of learning. When students dialogue, they connect learning from the past (stored information) with what they are currently trying to process. All of the senses are evoked because information that is to be remembered needs to make multiple connections to move beyond the working memory. The time for storing what is learned is relatively short, as most items in the working memory only stay there for about fifteen to twenty seconds.

It is necessary to avoid assuming that students, particularly those with any type of processing issue, can remember too many things (short-term) at the same time. Researchers have found that people can typically only learn about seven things at a time, but if we walk into a typical middle or high school classroom, we often see lists of twenty things to remember, or ten vocabulary words, fifteen facts and fifteen other non-related topics being discussed (Sousa, 2001; Wolfe, 2001). That is why strong inclusive classrooms focus on the *big idea* and what must be mastered for students to move on to the next concept or to pass the local and state assessments. In strong inclusive classrooms, teachers are aware of the latest research and literature, and ensure that their teaching reflects proven and promising practices rather than teaching only in the way they were taught or how they themselves learn.

Classrooms in which students with disabilities thrive have built-in levels of review. Once again, brain research clearly indicates that to remember something for more than just a few minutes, exposure or repetition must occur ten times or more (Jacobs-Connell, 2000). Therefore, starting with the big idea and then incorporating ongoing reviews, such as creating a visual timeline, can be helpful in ensuring information is stored in long-term memory. An excellent example of this is found with a teacher who realized that review was essential but found it difficult to schedule time for review because of the number of standards that needed to be taught each day. Therefore, in his classroom, students were asked to create a visual image of what they learned in a particular chapter or unit (this was in a competitive format and utilized the principles of cooperative learning). The best visual representation was selected and displayed on the wall. Before the class moved to the next chapter or unit, students were asked to talk about each visual image on the wall. This technique is wonderful to use with a subject such as social studies, where the lessons build over time, or with reading a chapter book. The visual images are then imprinted in the students' brains to bring back what they learned during unit or state assessments. In some states, teachers must remove all items from their walls before state testing, as was the case with this teacher. But before the state testing he said, "Although I have removed the visual images from the wall, if you just look where it was posted, I trust that your mind can recall that image to assist you with your test."

Finally, in a strong inclusive classroom, teachers understand the limitations of some students and teach to the level of knowledge a student is capable of mastering to avoid discouragement and increase pleasure in learning. Some students will have difficulty moving beyond the first, concrete level of knowledge (i.e. concrete steps). They need to see information in many ways and benefit from concrete examples in dialogue with their peers. With optimum support, many students in inclusive environments can move beyond the concrete level of knowing to the more representational or symbolic way of knowing. For students with processing and learning issues, recalling the representation or symbol may be difficult. Students who have difficulty in this area may need to be given a list of words to select from to answer fill-in the blank questions, or be allowed to describe (concrete) the image they can recall (sometimes in great detail), as they may not be able to recall the specific name.

Learning information at the abstract reasoning level can be difficult for many students and often is a major area of struggle for students with disabilities. Although difficult, this type of reasoning is used more commonly on a daily basis at the secondary level. The increased use of abstract reasoning often explains why some students are not diagnosed with a learning disability until the later school years. In strong inclusive classrooms where teachers are working together, often times special education teachers are excellent at taking abstract concepts and providing either symbolic or concrete examples to assist students in understanding the information that is presented.

Many times, when items are presented in multiple ways, students can reach higher levels of knowing. For example, if a student has an auditory processing disorder (he can hear but the language that comes in through his ears becomes garbled as his brain tries to interpret what he hears) and has a teacher who lectures, this student may be may prevented from moving beyond the concrete level. Yet if the lecture is accompanied by visual notes, pictures, and rich discussion with peers, and followed by several activities to enrich the discussion, the student's chance of gaining a higher level of knowledge greatly increases (Hardiman, 2001). The potential of understanding the lesson has increased for all students; students without an auditory issue might be able to learn in a non-lecture format, whereas the student with a disability is guaranteed to fail in a lecture-only learning environment. Teachers who teach to the range of learning differences embrace Dewey's philosophy of "look not for fault in the child but in the teaching of the child." There will always be concepts that are difficult or impossible for certain students to master, but that does not mean that learning cannot be improved if teachers clearly understand how students' brains learn and use that information to create a safe environment that embraces a wide range of learners.

The following list presents strategies for strong inclusive instruction. It can be used to reflect upon the current status of instruction in a school or classroom, or to identify types of instruction that might be incorporated into existing classroom strategies. Try ideas that you are comfortable with in your classroom, but at the same time be certain to not teach only to the way that you learn, or to get caught in a rut doing only what works for some and not trying ideas that might work for all learners.

Classroom Instruction Strategies
- Provide meaningful curriculum related to students' lives.
- Teach problem solving.
- Use projects or simulations.
- Ensure auditory and visual stimuli (at a minimum) in all lessons.
- Teach writing across all curriculum areas.
- Teach reading across all curriculum areas.
- Provide a safe environment for sharing emotions.
- Celebrate the unique differences of learners in the class.

Thinking and Attention Strategies
- Use mnemonic devices to aid memory.
- Encourage cognitive discourse to challenge thinking.
- Provide structure for peer teaching.
- Use hands-on activities.
- Provide real-life lessons and applications.
- Use novelty to engage students.
- Allow older students to collaborate with younger ones.
- Model skills you want students to exhibit.

Physical
- Allow movement every 10-15 minutes.
- Encourage students to move to music.
- Allow stretching breaks.
- Utilize various types of energizers such as 10 jumping jacks.
- Encourage end of the lesson goal setting on the move.
- Teach stress management techniques.
- Change locations (e.g., use station teaching).
- Get students out of their seats.

In strong inclusive schools, literacy skills are taught in each and every classroom, but more importantly, material is embraced that reflects a wide variety of learning styles and cultural backgrounds. For example, in a typical classroom, at the end of a chapter students are expected to write a summary of what they read or take a written test. However, in a class that is blended across disciplines and embraces reading and writing, instead of writing a traditional summary, students may be asked to create ten song titles that might be found on a CD that represents the lesson material, and to then write lyrics to a song that represents one of those titles. In collaboration with the art teacher, students are asked to create a cover for their CD, and in collaboration with the music teacher they might set their songs to some type of rhythm or music. For the final activity, the students are asked to share their songs. This activity could occur over several days or just a few days but, in this type of lesson, the learning is rich. Material is imprinted into the student's memory (chunked into small segments to ensure mastery) with the lesson focused on reading, summarizing, writing, art and music. This type of lesson activity is "Universally Designed" (Rose & Meyer, 2000; Rose, Meyer & Hitchcock, 2005) to meet the needs of a range of students. No matter what the needs of students with disabilities, accommodations can easily be made within this lesson (e.g., only make ten song titles, or just draw a picture, or just play the music).

When students with disabilities who are struggling readers are included in classrooms and do not receive ongoing structures to teach and enrich learning through modalities beyond reading or writing, a question emerges at the upper grade levels: Are the students unable to learn the content, or are they instead unable to read the material in a traditional way to learn the concepts that are presented? Students with disabilities must have material presented in their preferred learning style or area of strength. If a student has a reading disability, then material should be presented in another way such as talking, drawing, or scribing.

Exhibit 6.2 can be used by teachers to document the percentage of time spent during a particular lesson *telling, asking, showing* (which are all teacher-centered activities) and *doing* (student-centered learning). Once the information is gathered, teachers are challenged to think about how they might increase the amount of time students spend *doing*, which is a core concept related to student engagement, as presented in Chapter 5.

Exhibit 6.2 ~ Active Learning

Teacher *Telling*	Teacher *Asking*	Teacher *Showing*	Student *Doing*
_____%	_____%	_____%	_____%

Following this exercise, I typically ask teachers to name three to five subjects in which students with a range of disabilities were included twenty years ago. Responses typically include art, music, physical education, home economics and technical classes. Why were we able to include students twenty years ago into those classes, even at the secondary level? Students with disabilities were not any different at that time, but those classes were much higher in the activity or *doing* component. If students' learning in areas such as reading, writing, and math is to be enriched, then they must be helped to move from being passive consumers to active learners. We do not ask students to simply watch the teacher play basketball in physical education or to watch someone else cook in home economics. Rather, we allow them to be actively engaged in the tasks they are to complete. Similarly, they need to be engaged through reading, writing, and talking to learn.

If teachers spend ninety to one hundred percent of the time *telling* in their classes, then action needs to be taken. This does not mean that they have to immediately stop lecturing, but in each class they might try to lower the percentage of time spent *telling*, and increase the amount of student *doing*. The more activity-focused the lesson, the wider the range of adaptations and modifications that can be incorporated in both curriculum and instruction.

Practical Suggestions/Ideas from Research, Practice and Trends

The remainder of this chapter includes a variety of practical ideas to assist students and teachers in the areas of more active learning, writing, and reading. In strong secondary inclusive classrooms, students are highly engaged in their learning environments and they are reading, writing and speaking in each and every class, each and every day.

A wonderful book about secondary education is *The Big Picture* by Littky and Grabelle (2004). Its authors talk about a different kind of high school where differences are not a deficit, but an asset to learning. If students are absent, someone notices and is deeply concerned. Students are actively involved in their learning based on a different standard of education. This type of school allows students to be at the center of learning and embraces the needs of students with disabilities. One of my favorite quotes from the book (and there are many wonderful statements about thinking differently at the secondary level) is, "trust kids enough to allow them to help direct their own learning" (Littky and Grabelle,p. 106). This statement is applicable to secondary schools, especially in the case of students with disabilities. Unfortunately, it is uncommon to walk into a classroom where students with disabilities are empowered to talk about how they need to learn, what they are most interested in reading, or what they really want to learn. In great classrooms, teachers are the facilitators of learning and they realize that, although they may learn differently or behave differently, students with disabilities should still have a voice in this process called education.

The most powerful way secondary educators can increase motivation in secondary students is to give them a voice. In Michelle Fine's book, *Framing Dropouts* (1981), she talks about silencing and nurturing students' voices. As we think about students who are not motivated, we might want to consider if these students have a voice in their classrooms, schools, or communities.

Fostering Participation

Motivating secondary students to participate and giving them a voice in student-centered activities is a challenge. What follows are some techniques that I have found to be successful in encouraging participation.

- **Share with your neighbor** – Ask students to quickly turn to their neighbor and either list three things they have learned or share a two-sentence summary of the lesson.
- **Write and share a quiz question** - Ask students to share a quiz question they might have either verbally or in writing. Then, collect written questions and use them on your test, including the name of the creator of the question on the test.
- **Finger Signals** – Use this strategy with caution and be sure to explain explicitly which finger students are acceptable to use! For this strategy, tell students to raise one finger for yes and two for no; or, if you are doing a multiple choice review, instead of asking one student to respond, use this technique: make the ring finger A, two fingers B, three fingers C and four fingers D. Then you can assess the entire class instead of one student and all students will be more engaged.
- **Unison Response** – Instead of having one student answer a question, have all questions be answered in unison. Be certain to give students with disabilities plenty of processing time. I typically pose the question and then tell students to respond on the count of three.
- **Flashing answers** – With this strategy, all students write their answer on some type of response board and share their answers with the group or class. Dry erase boards work well, or you can buy gelboards from www.imagin eticsonline.com that look about like an etch-a-sketch and which students can put into binders. You also can buy Solo plastic plates and use these with a dry erase marker, or buy shower board from a local lumber yard and cut your own dry erase board. The cheapest option I have found is to acquire a sturdy box like a refrigerator box and then either use chalkboard spray paint or chalkboard contact paper to cover the box. Cut it into one foot squares and provide students with an old sock and a piece of chalk and they are set to respond.
- **Body Movement** - If students do not like to respond verbally to questions, ask them to do things such as stand up if you agree and sit down if disagree, or cross your arms if you think the answer is A and uncross your arms if you think it is B. These ideas allow all students to participate and provide some movement in the class.

- **Whip around or pass option** – This activity is great to use to start class. Each student is expected to either respond to a question or prompt. If they cannot or choose not to respond, they can then say pass. If the entire class passes on a question about a lecture they heard yesterday then a review of the content presented is probably needed.

Active participation in class as well as student engagement in reading and writing throughout the day are extremely important. In a recent article (Dieker & Little, 2005) my colleague and I wrote that "reading is not just for reading teachers anymore." In this time of higher and higher stakes testing, literacy instruction must be the job of everyone in the school. Strong inclusive schools embrace an interdisciplinary approach to instruction and know the value and importance of using areas such as art, music and physical education to assist students with special needs in the general education setting.

The first steps in ensuring that literacy is taught across the curriculum and that students have a voice are communicating across disciplines and talking to students. How can the concepts that are critical to students becoming strong readers be taught in mathematics and science or be incorporated into physical education, home economics or computer sciences? How can we relate students' interests to state standards? The answers are simple, but the structure is complex. Providing teachers with a curriculum framework that can be used for collaboration between general and special education, such as the one outlined in Chapter 4, Exhibit 4.3, can be a wonderful resource for elective teachers to tie together important concepts. Since all teachers have to align clear curricular goals related to state standards, identifying information that should be taught across the curriculum becomes easier and easier. Then, take these collective standards and ask students how they think they could best learn the standards. The richness of learning as well as the mastery of content increases greatly when students are empowered and actively participate in their education.

Reading and writing are taught everyday by every teacher in strong inclusive schools. For example, in one inclusive school, students are asked to write daily either a summary paragraph of what they learned yesterday or what they believe they will learn in the class today; then students are asked to read these statements aloud. A colleague in secondary English (Ousley, 2004) suggests that students should read, write, view, listen and discuss daily in strong classrooms. I would argue that these skills should be practiced in inclusive classrooms in all content areas.

Incorporating the skills of reading, writing, listening and discussing into the classroom allows teachers to address the needs of a range of different kinds of learners and allows all students to further practice oral and written communication, social skills and the critical areas of reading and writing. In inclusive classrooms, teachers focus on universally designed lessons that ensure the learning of all students and focus on Power Standards (those that are essential for mastery). Provided below are some excellent websites and ideas related to using reading and writing across content areas, as well as ideas for generating more writing while adding more pleasure to the process.

Writing Strategies
- **Look for opportunities for students to write**: e.g., job applications, freebies, letters, jokes, math problems, travel brochures, want ads, advice columns, book reviews.
- **Chat Room:** Get students to write by creating a chat room. Often students who do not participate in class will participate in written chatting. Be certain to set up rules to ensure positive interactions.
- **Be the Author:** Ask students to write journal entries or even a letter to the class from the author's perspective.
- **Cross-Age Penals:** Allow older students to write to first graders and then even the lowest level writer will look advanced in the eyes of the student who receives their letter.
- **Kamishibai** – This technique is one of my favorites as it embraces a range of learners and has built-in components of cooperative learning. Students work in groups of four, with each student given a role: sequencer, who determines how to depict the action of the story; an artist, who draws the pictures; a scriptwriter, who writes a script for each picture; and a performer, who acts out the scene. This technique is from Japanese culture. See the following Website for more information (http://www.kamishibai.com).

- **Pictures**: Use pictures to show students how to develop topic sentences and to illustrate the flow of a story. Cartoons are especially helpful.
- **Peer Editing with Credit :** Two peers edit a paper together and both receive credit for the improvement in the final paper.
- **Red/Green Pen:** When grading papers, circle errors in red and note good aspects of the writing in green. Then ask students why items were circled in green.
- **Expanded Sentences**: Start with simple sentences and, in cooperative groups, ask students to expand into larger sentences. Set a goal of a specific number of words per sentence.
- **Pass a Sentence**: Have students in cooperative groups write a starter sentences and then pass the starter sentence, asking each student to contribute to the paragraph.
- **Interviews**: Have students write interview questions and answer questions about numerous topics.
- **Vocabulary Journal**: For every subject area, have students keep a vocabulary journal of words and pictures to represent concepts from each content area. Then, teachers and students are encouraged to use these words across disciplines.
- **Written Assignments:** Use these strategies to help students with the writing process.
  - **COPS** (Schumaker, et al., 1982)
    - C = Capitalize the first word
    - O = Overall appearance
    - P = Punctuation
    - S = Spelling
  - **POWER** (Englert et al., 1992)
    - P = Planning
    - O = Organizing
    - W = Writing
    - E = Editing
    - R = Revising

Reading and Writing Websites
- **Cliffs Notes** — http://www.cliffsnotes.com — This site provides short summaries of stories that are excellent for students with disabilities to read instead of entire novels.

- **Spark Notes** — http://www.sparknotes.com — This site provides study guides related to classic novels and other areas often covered at the secondary level.
- **Novel Guide** — http://www.novelguide.com — This site is a free source for literary analysis on the web to assist students better understand both classic and contemporary text.
- **Free Book Notes** — http://www.freebooknotes.com — This site is a comprehensive guide to free book notes, free book summaries, literature notes, and study guides (like CliffsNotes) for over 1600 books, plays, and poems.
- **Pink Monkey** — http://www.pinkmonkey.com — This site features over 400 Free Book Notes, Study Guides, and Online Chapter Summary Notes.
- **Library of Congress** — http://www.loc.gov — This site is amazing and houses thousands of pictures and artifacts that can be used to enrich social studies lessons. Images from the site can be used for daily writing prompts.
- **Windows to the Universe** — http://www.windows.ucar.edu — *Windows to the Universe* is a user-friendly learning system for use by the general that covers public covering the Earth and space sciences. This site offers the same information at three levels — beginner, intermediate and advanced— and also translates text from English to Spanish with a click of a button. A great site for science or any subject area.
- **Text aloud** — http://www.readaloud.com — Provides books that can be read aloud. This site has a limited selection of secondary books, but is still an excellent resource to share with students and families and great to use for cross-age peer tutoring.
- **Text-to-speech web browsers** — These sites all provide tools that allow students to have text read to them:
  - **CAST eReader** — http://www.cast.org
  - **IBM's Home Page Reader** — http://www-3.ib.com/able/
  - **PwWebSpeak** — http://www.soundlinks.com/pwgen.htm
- **Babel Fish** — http://bablfish.altavista.com — Assists with translation of materials when English is not primary language.
- **Kidspiration/Inspiration** — http://www.inspiration.com — A great tool to help students organize notes for any

class or to use as a prewriting strategy. This tool basically creates semantic maps.

- **Paragraph Writing** — http://www.paragraphpunch.com — This website takes users through the actual steps of writing a basic paragraph.
- **iDictate** — http://www.idictate.com — For a small fee, students who need a scribe for their writing have a new resource. iDictate is a revolutionary blend of technology and human interaction that enables you to dictate any document using a telephone, fax machine, or dictation device, and then receive the completed job back for editing via e-mail.
- **Write "cyber biographies"** — http://www.geocities.com/bronx_tech/work.html — Students who access this site state who they are and the goals to which they aspire.
- **Telementoring** — http://www.tnellen.com/cybereng/ — Parents, community members and older students mentor students via the Internet.

Reading Strategies

In strong schools, students are interviewed, given a voice, and help shape how they learn and are how they are taught. They are part of the learning process and have input into what helps them learn and what does not. Students select materials they want to read and are provided with opportunities to do just that – read.

A strategy I strongly embrace for inclusive classrooms related to instruction for students who are different is one presented by Jobe and Dayton-Sakari (2002). They refer to students who are reluctant readers as "info-kids." Info-kids are not motivated by typical secondary literature such as *Romeo and Juliet* or *War nd Peace,* but instead read and are motivated by factoid-type books such as the *Genius World Book of Records,* or *Oh Yuk! The Encyclopedia of Everything Gross and Nasty* (Masoff, 2001). After reviewing Jobe and Dayton-Sakari's descriptions of info-kids, I found their description fits with many students with disabilities I have met or taught at the secondary level.

The 8 types of Info-Kids introduced by Jobe and Dayton-Sakari are:
- Info-kids who are outward focused,
- Info-kids who love facts,

- Info-kids who are hands-on,
- Info-kids who act or hide out,
- Info-kids who move to a different drummer,
- Info-kids who gravitate to the gross,
- Info-kids who picture the world,
- Info-kids who have novel perspectives.

Strong inclusive classrooms embrace the unique interests of all students, including info-kids and students with disabilities, and understand the strong correlation between the motivation to read and the ability or inability to read. Info-Kids are given the option of reading nonfiction books that can be very engaging and at the same time meet the needs of getting students to process more text. In reading research, there is a direct correlation between the amount of print a child consumes and their reading level (Guthrie, Wigfield, Metsala & Cox, 1999).

Too many times at the secondary level we assume chapter books or classic novels are the way to get students to consume text, but I strongly suggest using nonfiction fact books as well as young adolescent literature to motivate, enrich and increase the reading levels of students with disabilities. For a list of great info-kids books, see the book by Jobe and Dayton-Sakari ,and refer to Appendix A at the end of this book.

In schools and classrooms that embrace all kinds of learners, teachers understand that the amount of text is more important than type of material. They also understand that students need to read material not just in their English class but in all subject areas. That type of reading is exactly the way Info-kids like to read; not just from cover to cover but from bits and pieces of knowledge. For this reason, the World Wide Web is a part of strong inclusive class-rooms as it relates to the preferences of the info-kid. Consider whether a student can navigate the Internet and then ask, is that student unable to read, or is he no longer motivated to read the material assigned in thesecondary classrooms?

Related to the struggling reader, the following list provides ideas from great teachers for bringing about more effective teach-ing and/or more pleasant learning experiences.
- **Modeling** — Teacher reads a passage and models strate-gies she/he utilized to better understand the text.

- **Think Aloud** — Teacher thinks aloud about how he/she derived meaning from the text that was read, or asks a student to do so.
- **Creative Debate** — Students are asked to take on characters in a story (or in content areas or other concepts presented). One third of the students take on one character and sit face-to-face in a circle with students who take on the other character while the final third observes. Then, after a ten to fifteen minute debate, the observers share a short verbal, written or pictorial summary of what occurred.
- **Reciprocal Questioning** (Palinscar & Brown, 1984) — In this procedure, the student and teacher take turns leading a dialogue about the text that was read. There are typically four phases 1) Summarizing — Learners read a passage and identify "Big Ideas;" 2) Questioning — Questions are posed; 3) Clarifying — Readers focus on unfamiliar vocabulary and puzzling concepts; 4) Predicting — Students use all the information available in the reading, including pictures and text structure, to determine what might happen next.
- **Tall Friends** — Secondary students engage in cross-age tutoring of primary students to practice the alphabet and consonant sounds, or use word-sort activities to group words according to particular phonemes. The student tutors get reinforcement of basic skills while working with younger students. Typically, this activity is tied in with a daily journal that tutors keep to the record the progress of their primary students. An excellent example of this is a book entitled, *Succeeding in Reading: Complete Cross-Age Tutoring Program* created by Dean and Harper (2005). This book provides a complete step-by-step guide for cross-age tutoring.
- **Think, Pair, Share** — Students write down personal reactions, then give their written thoughts to a partner, who writes a reaction to that student's statement.
- **Author's Chair**: Allow a student to act as the author and answer questions from the students who are reading the book.
- **Predictions** (Mathes, 1994) — Students are grouped into pairs with one student selected to read first. The pair proceeds as follows:
    — The student who will read predicts what will happen.

— The student not reading asks the reader if the prediction came true. This statement is followed by asking why or why not.

— The student who reads is asked to summarize what is read using ten words or less (the nonreader counts the # of words).

— Students switch roles and repeat.

- **Framing a Story** — Present story frames before students read a passage. Have students predict the information that will fit into the blanks. After students read the passage, ask them to confirm or reject their predictions.

- **Spirit Reading** — A student continues to read until the "spirit moves" them to stop and then any other student who the "spirit moves" can start reading.

- **Word Sorts** — When introducing vocabulary, ask students to sort the words into categories (either categories you provide or categories the students create).

- **Auto Summarize** — Use Microsoft Word's auto summarize feature to put the text into a modified format. This function can be found under the tool bar.

- **Essential Words** — As students read a passage, have them cross out irrelevant information until only the ten most important words from the passage remain.

- **Draw a Picture of the Story** — Students are asked to demonstrate comprehension by drawing a picture or pictograph of what they have read.

- **Book Reviews**:
    — Have students act as reviewers for books and give ratings (thumbs up or thumbs down);

    — Have students create a short film featuring their review of books, then put these reviews in the library for other students to use to select books they want to read;

    — Have a review column in the school newspaper.

- **Commercials**: Have students write and videotape a commercial related to a book they have read. Create slogans or campaigns or even a song in collaboration with the art and music teachers.

- **Act out the story**: Students are asked to act out what they have read either in a group, in pairs, or by themselves. Ask the drama teacher to work collaboratively on this project.

- **Develop a timeline** — Students are to develop a timeline of the events that occurred in the story or across chapters. Put visual images of the timeline on the wall and review weekly.

- **Story Retell** — Students are asked to retell the story in their own words.
- **For, With and By** — Read a passage of about 100 words to the student twice (for), then ask them to read it with you (with). Finally, have them read the same passage by themselves (by) (Wilber, 2000).
- **Draw a Name** — Student's names are randomly drawn from a pile and the student whose name is called must read aloud. Because they do not know when/if their name will be called, students are forced to pay attention. If there is a student with special needs in the class, you can rehearse a passage with him ahead of time (make sure to call on him to read the passage he has pre-learned).
- **Stuffed Animal Reading:** Have students practice reading aloud to stuffed animals.
- **Popcorn** — Students read aloud and say "popcorn," followed by a peers' name, to pass off to another readers.
- **Five Finger Rule** — Suggest students use the following rule in making reading selections: if, after reading the first couple of pages, you know all the words except five and can ask yourself and answer five questions about what you have read, this is probably an appropriate book to read.
- **Comprehending Text** — As students read text, encourage them to use these strategies to assist with comprehension:
  - **RAP** (Schumaker, Denton, & Deshler, 1984)
    - R = Read a paragraph
    - A = Ask yourself a question
    - P = Put the main idea and details in your own words
  - **KWL**
    - K = What you already Know
    - W = what you Want to know
    - L = what you Learned
  - **SCROL** (Grant, 1993)
    - S = Survey the headings
    - C = Connect
    - R = Read the text
    - O = Outline
    - L = Look back

— **POSSE** (Englert & Mariage, 1991)
    P = Predict Ideas
    O = Organize ideas
    S = Search for the structure
    S = Summarize the main ideas
    E = Evaluate your understanding

In summary, every teacher in strong inclusive secondary schools uses proven and promising practices. Instruction is provided that is differentiated, multi-sensory, and involves active student learning. Various types of reading materials are found in the classroom and students are given opportunities to use reading and writing skills across the curriculum. Everyone in the school assumes it is their job to teach reading and writing in a manner that is pleasant and effective for both teacher and student. Most importantly, students who read and write at all levels are accepted and expected to learn and be successful. The expectation of success for all in the general education setting is what sets apart a school that embraces the philosophy of inclusion versus just another school where only certain students are able to learn.

Reflective Questions

1. How is reading incorporated in all areas of our school's curriculum? How could we increase the amount of time in spent in various content areas practicing and honing reading and writing skills?
2. How is laughter and active learning embraced in our classroom or school?
3. What one suggestion for incorporating reading and/or writing into the content area can we try with our students?
4. How do other subject area teachers take ownership for the content mandated for mastery in core curricular areas?
5. What types of materials beyond traditional classic works are provided to encourage students to engage in reading?

References

D'Arcangelo, M. (1998). The brains behind the brain. *Educational Leadership*, 56(2), 20-25.

Dean, N. & Harper, C. (2005). *Succeeding in reading: Complete cross-age tutoring program*. Maupin House: Gainesville, FL.

Dieker, L. & Little, M (2005). Secondary Reading: Not just for reading teachers anymore. *Intervention in School and Clinic, 40*, 276-283.

Englert, C. S. & Mariage, T. V. (1991). Making students partners in the comprehension process: Organizing the reading "POSSE". *Learning Disability Quarterly*, 14(2), 123-138.

Englert, C. S., Raphael, T. E., & Anderson, L. M (1992). Socially mediated instruction: Improving students' knowledge and talk about writing. *Elementary School Journal*, 92(4), 411-449.

Feinstein, S. (2004) *Secrets of the teenage brain*. San Diego, CA: The Brain Store.

Fine, M. (1991). *Framing dropouts: Notes on the politics of an urban high school*. Albany: SUNY Press.

Grant, R. (1993). Strategic Training for Using Text Headings to Improve Students' Processing of Content. *Journal of Reading, 36(6), 428-488.*

Gurian, M. & Stevens, K. (2004). Closing achievement gaps with boys and girls in mind. *Educational Leadership*, 62(3), 21-26.

Guthrie, J. T., Wigfield, A., Metsala, J. L., & Cox, K. E. (1999). Motivationanl and cognitve predictors of text comprehension and reading amount. *Scientific Studies of Reading*, 3(3), 231-256.

Hardiman, M. M. (2001). Connecting brain research with dimensions of learning. *Educational Leadership*, 59(3), 52-55.

Jacobs-Connell, J. D. (2000). *Brain-based teaching.* Classroom Leadership, 4(3), 6-7.

Jensen, E. (1998). *Teaching with the brain in mind.* Alexandria, VA: Association for Supervision and Curriculum Development.

Jobe, R. & Dayton-Sakari, M. (2002). *Info-Kids: How to use nonfiction to turn reluctant readers into enthusiastic learners.* Ontario: Pembroke.

Kindlon, D. & Thompson, M. (1999). *Raising Cain: Protecting the emotional life of boys.* Ballantine Books: NY.

Littky, D. & Grabelle, S. (2004). *The Big Picture: Education is Everyone's Business.* Alexandria, VA: ASCD.

Masoff, J. (2001). *Oh yuck! The encyclopedia of everything nasty.* NY: Workman Publishing.

Mastropieri, M. & Scruggs, T. E. (2005). Feasibility and Consequences of Response to Intervention: Examination of the Issues and Scientific Evidence as a Model for the Identification of Individuals with Learning Disabilities, *Journal of Learning Disabilities*, 38(6), 525–531.

Mathes, P. (1994). Increasing strategic reading practice with Peabody classwide peer tutoring. *Learning Disabilities Research and Practice, 9(1), 44-48.*

Ousley, D. (2004). Alternative assessment and the brown bag exam. *Focus on Middle School, 3(4)* 1-5.

Palinscar, A. S. & Brown, A. L. (1984). Reciprocal teaching of comprehension-fostering and comprehension-monitoring activities. *Cognition and Instruction,* 1(2), 117-175.

Pipher, M (1995). *Reviving Ophelia: Saving the selves of adolescent girls.* Ballantine Books: NY.

Pollack, W. S. (1999). *Real boys: Rescuing our sons from the myths of boyhood.* Owl Books.

Rose, D. H., & Meyer, A. (2000). Universal Design for Learning. *Journal of Special Education Technology* 15(1): 67-70.

Rose, D. H., Meyer, A., & Hitchcock, C. (2005). *The universally designed classroom: Accessible curriculum and digital technologies.* Cambridge, MA: Harvard Education Press.

Schumaker, J. B., Denton, P. H., & Deshler, D. D. (1984). *The paraphrasing strategy.* Lawrence, KS: The University of Kansas.

Schumaker, J.B., Deshler, D.D., Alley, G.R., Warner, M.M., Clark, F.L., & Nolan, S. (1982). Error monitoring: A learning strategy for improving adolescent academic performance. In W. M. Cruickshank & J. W. Lerner (Eds.), *Coming of age: Vol. 3 The best of ACLD* (pp. 170-183). Syracuse, NY: Syracuse University Press.

Sousa, D. A. (2001). *How the special needs brain learns.* Thousand Oaks, CA: Corwin Press, Inc.

Sprenger, M. B. (2002). *Becoming a "wiz" at brain-based teaching.* Thousand Oaks, CA: Corwin Press, Inc.

Sultanoff, S. M. (1995). What is humor. *Therapeutic Humor*, 9 (3), 1-2.

Wilber, P. (2000). *Reading Rescue 1-2-3 : Raise Your Child's Reading Level 2 Grades with This Easy 3-Step Program.* Prima Publishing: Roseville, CA.

Wolfe, P. S. (2001). *Brain matters.* Alexandria, VA: Association for Supervision and Curriculum Development.

Chapter 7

Improving Grading and Student Assessment

Many students in our schools today experience difficulty with the reading and writing process. This is especially true for students with disabilities. Therefore, assessments that focus only on reading and writing serve to remind these students of their difficulties and their lack of success in school. For parents, results from such assessments reinforce the problems created by this world of paper and pencil tests. As a parent of a child with a disability, I can attest to this fact! Assessment in general at the secondary level has been and will continue to be a challenge, no matter what system we use. In a perfect world, all letter grades would disappear, and all general and special educators would agree on an alternate way of addressing the unique learning and assessment needs of all students. In schools that celebrate all learners, the administration and staff understand why a different way of measuring success is critical.

Grading is one of the first issues that should be addressed in both inclusive classrooms and inclusive schools — so why have I not addressed this issue until Chapter 7? Because, without the right school-wide philosophy and classroom environments that embrace teaching a different kind of learner, it is very difficult to confront this issue. Schools that have successfully included students with a range of special needs have addressed grading school-wide to facilitate classroom teachers in teaming or including students. Strong inclusive schools adopt the perspective of a *glass half full.* Rather than assuming that certain students cannot learn, teachers recognize that certain students cannot demonstrate what they know through traditional means.

Paper and pencil tests are dictated by most state education departments, but children should not fail in school merely because they fail at test-taking. Motivation and emotion permeate all aspects of learning. Students with disabilities begin to resent school if they are always assessed through their weaknesses. By the time children with disabilities get to the secondary level, they frequently resist anything having to do with school because they are tired of failing or just surviving. Often, when they reach this point, they no longer try because they are constantly asked to focus only on what they cannot do.

So, how do we build upon reading and writing skills, encourage motivation, and still assess learning in a less traditional manner? As mentioned in Chapter 2, answers to the questions of grading and student assessment are complex. Although teachers must deal with these issues within the classroom, a school-wide structure for assessment and grading is necessary, particularly in co-teaching situations, as lack of this can cause disagreements and stress for the teachers and the students. Addressing the issues of assessment and grading is another opportunity to reinforce the concept, *Fair is Not Always Equal.* If fair really means everyone gets what they need, then our current system, wherein everyone is expected to show that they learned in the same manner, is clearly unfair. Teachers in strong inclusive secondary schools realize this and create a variety of ways for students to learn and to assess their learning.

Before starting to talk about day-to-day assessment, it is important to remember that teachers have available to them a plethora of assessment information about students with disabilities. General education teachers should not be reticent to review the files of students with disabilities to determine their areas of strength and areas of concern.

An Emerging Trend: Response to Intervention (RTI)

An emerging practice in the field of special education is Response to Intervention, better known as RTI. Used most often in the field of learning or behavioral disabilities, RTI focuses on assessing whether meaningful change is produced when a specific intervention is used with a student. The intent of this process is to prevent students from failing in the early years of school. Governed by the reauthorization of IDEA in 2004, RTI is a different approach from the traditional way of diagnosing learning disabilities based upon psychological testing and the discrepancy between intelligence and achievement. Instead of using a deficit model that views the problem as residing within the student, RTI requires that appropriate reading interventions be documented before a child can be referred to special education. The burden falls on general educators to provide solid reading instruction in the primary grades. Very specifically, IDEA provides that children cannot be identified as having a disability when the determinating factor is the lack of appropriate instruction in reading, based upon the essential components of reading as defined in the No Child Left Behind Act. The most notable aspect of RTI is that it offers a method for assessing the "opportunity to learn" by incorporating the notion of early intervention and/or pre-referral strategies. It reduces inappropriate referrals and identification of students while establishing a prevention model for all students in a school

From the vantage point of secondary education, the move away from the discrepancy model can prevent the potentially harmful effects of delaying intervention until a student's achievement is so low that there is no "catching up." If implemented effectively in the primary grades, RTI may well alleviate some of the major problems that are presently caused by the difficulties that secondary level students experience with the reading process. Also, the students in secondary classrooms will potentially be more effective learners who have benefited from targeted intervention. Secondary teachers may also be able to use lessons learned from RTI to better inform their instruction. However, secondary educators in the field question if the model itself will work at the secondary level, as IDEA 2004 states that almost 30 years of research and experience has demonstrated that the education of children with disabilities can be made more effective by providing incentives for whole-school approaches.

I foresee potential struggles with RTI stemming from the lack of a collaborative structure at the secondary level. From my earlier work with child study or intervention assistance teams, I recognize that the challenges of gathering data across teachers at the secondary level to assess the effectiveness of an intervention can be difficult. In small learning communities, RTI may be possible, but in large, disjointed schools, determining if an intervention is working across seven or eight teachers a day may be a greater challenge. As stated by well-known secondary researchers Mastropieri and Scruggs (2005), "The question of application of RTI at the middle and early high school years as a procedure to identify students with LD is significant and remains unclear at present" (p. 527). Despite the promise of RTI to prevent labels and provide more effective responses to the needs of elementary students, unless radical reform in our ability to assess and gather data across numerous teachers in often large schools occurs nationwide at the secondary level, this type of tool may have its limitations for impacting secondary students with disabilities.

Assessment/Grading Options

In an effort to simplify this challenge, I am providing solutions and examples, based upon my numerous visits to and observations in real schools as well as my lecturing across the country, of what is being done to uniquely assess and report student learning. These same ideas can be used at the classroom level, but adopting a system school-wide that embraces a wider range of learners and learning styles will not just be beneficial to the students with disabilities, but can be helpful to all students (Obiakor, Obi, & Algozzine, 2001).

Innovative schools embrace a variety of tools to assist students in self-assessing so that they are better prepared to advocate for their needs. This includes helping students develop a strong sense of self, the ability to select tasks that target their strength, and skills to advocate for needs in their areas of weakness. These are critical skills not just for school, but also for life.

Standards-based reports cards: With a strong movement in all states to have clearly articulated curriculum standards, moving to a standards-based system is easier than ever (Stecker & Fuchs, 2000; Walsh & Matlock, 2000). However, determining mastery of these standards at the secondary level for over 120 students per teacher could become a paperwork nightmare. In response, some schools are starting to use a system that shows the level of mastery of the standards by indicating levels such as "emerging" or "mastered" for each of the state standards for which they are responsible. This model is far superior to models in which a simple letter grade represents an entire cluster of state standards in a specific subject area. The standards-based report documents the students' level of performance, and enables current and future teachers as well as the students and their families, to understand where there has been progress and what skills still need attention. In contrast, letter grades are frequently vague and lack clarity as to what skills are missing, providing little direction as to areas to focus on to build a student's skills.

IEP Grading: Another student assessment method parallels the mandates in IDEA. Students with disabilities must show progress on their IEP goals as often as reports are completed for their non-disabled peers. Some schools are choosing to use this information to provide either a partial credit for a student's final grade, or are reporting this progress as a separate grade on the report card. Yet in our current grading system, unless they are on an alternative assessment, students with disabilities are expected to meet all of the standards of the general education curriculum; then we spend time and energy creating an Individualized Education Programs (IEP) to ensure the students' needs are met in the general education curriculum; we then take all of this work and compile it into a single letter grade based upon the same standards for all students. Even though five to ten years earlier we determined that these students with identified disabilities were not the same learners as everyone else, we still use the same standards to assess them. In really strong inclusive schools or districts, we see a system that embraces and celebrates both the general education curriculum as well as the student's progress on IEP goals.

Exhibit 7.1 provides a tool that teachers can use to track students' IEP goals and report data on their progress towards these goals. A simple spreadsheet is used with students' names across the top and IEP goals down the side. A check is placed in appropriate cells to show that this specific goal is on the student's IEP. Then, students' performance related to their goals can be determined using simple data collection tools (e.g., frequency counts, observational data). This data then becomes the basis for quarterly reports that are provided to parents, or it may be merely partial consideration for the student's final grade.

One team of secondary teachers uses this form to create a weighted grading system that provides students with disabilities credit for meeting their IEP goals. This team shared that using this system allowed everyone to have a one page summary of goals, thus helping them as a team to focus more on students' IEP goals. The team decided to only write IEP goals that can be measured or met in the general education setting. They also found more consistency across teachers, and they were able to more easily articulate the goals for each student. Finally, and most importantly, students were both rewarded and held accountable for meeting their IEP goals as well as the general education standards.

Exhibit 7.1 ~ IEP Tracking and Grading Form

	Latasha	Jolee	Bill	Sean	Matt	Quincy	Deon	Tyler
Respects Others and Property	✓					✓		
Positive Attitude/ Behavior	✓	✓				✓		
Completes Tasks	✓					✓	✓	
On-Task	✓		✓	✓	✓	✓		
Homework	✓		✓	✓			✓	✓
Assignment Book	✓		✓	✓				
Initiates Task	✓		✓					
Breaks down and completes task on-time					✓		✓	
Seeks support when needed - academic - medical					✓			
Organizes Materials								✓
Checks Work								✓
Follows Directions								✓

Combined Grading: In this model, two teachers determine grades. There may be two separate grades or a combined single grade. Either way, teachers must understand and accept the process at the beginning of the semester, and students, as well as families, must also be very clear about the methodology of the grading from the start (Laframboise, Epanchin, Colucci, & Hocutt, 2004). Many times, the decision to use this type of model is considered at the end of the marking period, which can often cause conflict (even at times unspoken conflict) between general and special educators. Also, students with disabilities and their families often are not informed about how this grading system will work. When I interview students with disabilities about their grades they often share that they receive "magical grades." When asked to explain what the student means, he goes on to articulate that he knew he had a D or even a failing grade in a class but somehow at the end of the semester he magically receives letter grades of a C.

Why is receiving a passing grade a problem? First and foremost, it is a problem because the student and his family did not clearly understand how he was being evaluated. Secondly, for this change to "magically" occur at the end of the period means the way in which students with disabilities would be assessed was not determined prior to the start of the semester, and may not have been clear to the general or special education teacher.

The following example of a scenario that might occur in a typical secondary school illustrates the issues with combined grading. A student with a disability in a general education setting gives 150% in effort and does academic work at the C level, this representing his personal best. The general educator determines the student gets a C, but the special educator advocates for a B based on effort. In a perfect world, both skills would be reflected in a format other than letter grades. However, in the real world, teachers often compromise and give the student a C+ or B-. Some would argue this report card should reflect an A, since the student gained more skills in that semester than any other student in the class. Giving students credit for effort is fine if this level of effort can be clearly defined. However, skill level must also be reflected (perhaps two different grades are given). It is also possible for only one grade to be given but both teachers, as well as the student and his family, should clearly understand the grading criteria at the beginning of the semester so that at the end there is no need for "magic."

Let's look at another example. In my home district, students get letter grades on their report cards, but these grades are put in boxes that indicate "letter reflects performance below grade level." Is this system better than receiving an F in reading again? I would argue a report card with a B "below grade level" is not as good as one that is a standards-based report card; but, it is better than a system that ensures each semester students and their family are guaranteed only one outcome — failure.

The troublesome nature of this type of grading is obvious and reinforces the need to ensure that there is clarity for everyone — teachers, students and families — about the specific criteria that are being used. Without a clear discussion, conflict and confusion exist or even worse, a student's only outcome because of a disability is an F — for failure.

Rubric Report Cards: A rubric is a scoring guide in the form of a set of guidelines that provide clear performance criteria, in developmental order, that have an accompanying rating scale. As such, they provide great clarity as to what is expected; students and teachers understand what skills need to be mastered. One school uses rubric report cards with attached rubrics to provide clarity as to what an actual score meant. IEPs were also written with rubrics so that scores on these goals can be included with the report card. A tool that can be very helpful in promoting the use of rubric report cards is www.rubistar.4teachers.org. This website provides tools to assist teachers in creating rubrics or adopting ones that are already developed. Rubrics are a wonderful tool that increase overall student performance and at the same time forces greater clarity in what is valued in student learning outcomes. Schools that have embraced this model find it to be a much more meaningful way to evaluate learning. It is also easier for parents to clearly understand the skills their child has mastered and what more their child needs to do to move up in rubric scores. Rubric systems are unlike a letter grade system where, if a student gets a B, parents simply know that their child needs to do *more stuff better,* but may not understand what skill(s) their child still needs to master. If a rubric system is used, then parents know what skill level their child has achieved and are aware of the next level that needs to be addressed.

In one school, special educators use the low rubric scores of individual students with disabilities to create IEP goals (with rubrics attached) to assist students in areas of weakness. With a rubric system, the missing skills are much more clearly identified than in a traditional grading system. These missing skills can then be taught to raise rubric scores. Using the traditional grading system, if a student receives a grade of a C, this letter grade does not tell the special educator, student, or parents what needs to be improved. Yet a rubric score of a one should tell students, their parents, and teachers what additional skills are needed to raise that score to a two or three.

Rubric scores also can be used to determine class rank (calculated in a similar fashion to a letter grade system), which is a very real and important issue at the secondary level. Exhibit 7.2 provides an example of a rubric report card format that represents IEP goals, curricular standards, and important social skills needed for success

Exhibit 7.2 ~ Sample Rubric Report Card format

	1st Quarter	2nd Quarter	3rd Quarter
Social Studies			
Math			
Science			
Interpersonal Skills			
Language Arts			
Foreign Language			
Behavior			
Public Speaking			
Enthusiasm for Learning			
IEP Goals - On-task			
Bringing needed materials			
Participating in class			
Turning in Homework			

Comments

in life. The variety of skills represented on this report card shows the deficiency of our current grading system in which a simple letter reflects a narrowly defined measure of success — and typically completion of lots of work — not necessarily skills acquired.

Exhibits 7.3 and 7.4 are sample rubrics used in a secondary inclusive school.

Exhibit 7.3 ~ Sample Interpersonal Rubric

1. Identifies work group; recognizes value s/he brings to the group; knows basic group rules

2. Identifies group roles; recognizes the contribution of others, knows the rules of the group; cooperates with the group's decision

3. Identifies the goals of his/her group; follows the leadership of the group; follows the rules of the group; accepts thoughts of other group members

4. Contributes thoughts, ideas and energy to the group effort; communicates ideas to the group; provides direction to the group; negotiates differences of opinion

5. Takes personal responsibility as a member of the group to accomplish tasks; justifies a position to others; assists the group in making compromises; understands the concerns of other group members

6. Takes personal responsibility for accomplishing team goals; uses encouragement, persuasion and motivation to direct team; uses strengths of others to support team efforts; works effectively with others regardless of personal differences

Exhibit 7.4 ~ Sample Social Studies Rubric

1. Identifies materials

2. Manipulates materials to find information; demonstrates an awareness of various cultures and people

3. Uses appropriate material to apply knowledge of currently studied topics; demonstrates awareness and appreciation of various cultures and people; identifies connections in historical events

4. Uses appropriate materials to extend and refine knowledge of currently studied topics; demonstrates an appreciation for and can evaluate differences in various cultures; identifies connections between historical events and self

5. Selects specific material to analyze knowledge of currently studied topics; exhibits an awareness and appreciation of various cultures; formulates connections between historical events, present society and self

6. Incorporates various materials to exhibit and evaluate currently studied topics and understands how these topics relate to the past, present and future within the students' own life and the greater society

Checklist Grading: Checklist grading can be used in combination with a letter grade system or as a stand-alone system. Checklists are created for each class to represent levels of proficiency for students in that subject area. The number of skills that are accomplished are then turned into a letter grade. This system can be used to blend modified grading and a letter grade system (e.g., 8 skills equals 80%). In one school, these modified checklists were presented to students at the beginning of the semester and then attached to the report card system. When this was done, parents knew exactly what the grade their child received represented. For some students with disabilities, their grades reflected perhaps five academic skills and five social skills, but again clarity was provided for teachers, parents and students.

Exhibitions: Exhibitions are a type of assessment used to demonstrate learning. Just because schools have always used letter grades, or just because schools send home report cards and have conferences twice a year, does not mean this is the best way to support the learning of all students. In strong inclusive schools, data are collected on all aspects of the environment, including student grade performance and parent attendance at conferences. A great way to increase student and parent involvement is by using a tool called exhibition assessment. With this type of assessment the teacher simply outlines the skills a student must demonstrate to show mastery of the content area (e.g., state standards). Then, students are told they can demonstrate their knowledge any way they might choose, from writing a play, to creating artwork, to writing an essay. Basically, the diversity of how the learning is assessed is as diverse as the learners in the classroom. Parents are then invited not to a parent-teacher conference, but instead to a performance where students exhibit what they have learned. One student might read excerpts from the paper he wrote, while another displays her art and a group of students acts out a segment of the play they created. This type of assessment technique embraces a wide range of learners and allows students to work in their area of strength.

Portfolios: This type of assessment is required for students on alternative assessments in most states, but there are schools and even universities that use only a portfolio system. Typically, these portfolios are combined with some type of rubric that is used for students to set their own specific academic or behavioral goals. This type of goal setting is what is needed for success as an adult. The process of sharing specific examples of work with families can very positively effect students' self-esteem. Although this is a wonderful system to use at the middle and high school level, it can be more difficult because of managing the process of selecting meaningful work and organizing material across teachers on a regularly scheduled basis. However, schools that successfully use portfolios believe it is well worth the effort as they embrace the diversity of the students in their schools.

Student-Centered Conferences – Many schools that are inclusive also realize that partnerships with parents are critical and that that traditional conferences at the secondary level may not produce the quality of partnerships that are most desired. Instead of having parent-teacher conferences, many schools find the middle and high school level is a great place to introduce parent to student conferences. Parents are more likely to attend a conference led by their own child. Additionally, this type of conference helps students learn how to accurately assess their own strengths and weaknesses. This technique also prepares students for future work-place self-evaluation.

At one school utilizing this assessment method, the student to parent conferences focus on students sharing with their parents/guardian what they feel they have accomplished and what they hope to accomplish in the next quarter. Using this type of conferencing for students with disabilities not only allows them to talk with their parents about positive aspects of school, but also encourages them to more fully understand their own disabilities and to advocate for their needs. In one middle school that transitioned from parent-teacher conferences to student-to-parent conferences, parents' participation in conferences skyrocketed. Why might this be? Every year (typically two to three times a year) parents are asked to come to school to talk about their child. During the elementary years, parents hear over and over and over again about the skills their child is still lacking. When teachers complain that parents do not come to conferences when their child gets older, the question that should be asked is, "Why should they?" Many parents of children with disabilities can predict that the same record will be played over and over again, just with a different voice. Yet ask a parent to come and talk with their own child or see their child perform, and the tune changes. No longer is there fear of hearing about failure but instead hopeful anticipation of hearing from their child. As an example, compare the attendance of parents at school plays or basketball games to that of parent conferences. If there is a significant difference, the problem may not be that the parents are not committed, but rather that they need a good reason to attend. By providing a change in the structure that enables them to learn more about their child's strengths as well as weaknesses, parents have added incentive to participate in conferences.

No matter what type of grading system is adopted in class-rooms or schools, there will always be an exception to the structure. With IDEA 2004 focused on allowing another 2% of students with disabilities to be exempted from traditional assessments, classroom teachers should be prepared to have two to three students each year who will not fit the mold of traditional grading. If a school has already moved away from a traditional A, B, C system, then accom-modating these two or three students will be easy. If not, then similar to the approach found in a Positive Behavioral Intervention Support (PBIS) school, when there might be students who do not fit even the most structured and consistent behavioral system, a team may need to be set up to talk about ways to adapt and modify grading for this subset of students. In his book *Solving the Grading Puzzle for Students with Disabilities* (2003), Dennis Munk argues there will always be some students who need unique grading systems. By continuing to give students an F grade, schools ensure that these students give up and drop out of school. We actually know that there is a direct correlation to students failing freshman algebra and dropping out of school (Balfanz & Legters, 2004). Schools that are nurturing know that the growth of students, especially students with disabilities who may only show a year's worth of growth every three years, cannot be evaluated by a simple grade. They celebrate students by using alternative ways to both reward them and to show how they have mastered skills at this level.

The questions that follow were proposed by Meltzer, et al (1996). They should be used when secondary schools are rethink-ing their grading structure at either the school or classroom level. These types of questions should be considered prior to the start of the semester, and should be revisited at least each semester as new students with a range of learning and behavioral needs come into class. If the class is co-taught, then both teachers should be involved with these considerations on a regular basis.

Questions to Ask Related to Grading
• Are we explicit about the grading policy?
• Do we use multilevel grading?

- Do we give credit for participation?
- Do we evaluate student performance in a variety of ways?
- Do we embrace multiple intelligences?

Additional proactive questions posed by Cohen (1982) that special educators should address with their general education counterparts before the start of the semester, include the following:

Additional Grading Questions
- Who is responsible for assigning the report card grade?
- Should the grade be based on the discrepancy between the student's actual and potential performance, or between the actual performance and grade level expectancy?
- What type of grading feedback should be given on a daily basis?
- What type of descriptive annotation will best complement the system's report card grading procedure?
- Whom should a parent contact to discuss a grade?

Day to Day Assessment

Another issue that has to be considered in inclusive schools and classrooms is the day-to-day assessment tools used and how students are prepared for these assessments. In an inclusive classroom, both the tools and their adaptations must be considered. The following section provides tools and tips to consider related to assessment items for a traditional classroom at the secondary level.

Some excellent websites to consider related to assessment are:
- Quia — http://www.quia.com — Assists in making and redesigning quizzes.
- QuizStar — http://quizstar.4teachers.org — A free service that allows teachers to give online quizzes.
- Fun Brain — http://www.funbrain.com — Lots of fun assessment types of games and tools.l
- Quiz Center — http://school.discovery.com/quizcenter/quizcenter.html — Allows teachers to administer and grade quizzes online.
- Easy Test Maker — http://www.easytestmaker.com — Allows teachers to make test in varying formats at no cost.

These tools can make the job of creating tests easier but often times secondary level students with disabilities have two issues arise related to day-to-day assessments. The first focuses on the need for extended time to complete tests. Although this accommodation is an important one, it can become problematic. For example, at the secondary level, students who take advantage of this option and have three tests in a day could be at school until midnight. Second, time may not be available for tests to be modified, especially if new material is adapted or general educators do not plan far enough in advance. Despite these challenges, Exhibit 7.5 provides examples of other types of assessments that might be considered, with a short description provided for each. These tools can help provide a bigger picture of a students' true performance in various content areas.

Alternative Assessments

Exhibit 7.5 ~ Types of Alternative Assessments

Assessment Techniques	Use in Inclusive Schools
Observation	Observe a teacher or ask someone to observe you interacting with the student. During the observation, data is gathered to use for assessment purposes. This tool is often used to gather data for behavioral goals in co-taught settings.
Work Sample Analysis (see Exhibit 7.6)	Use samples of students' work to directly examine areas in need of remediation. Also use this analysis to allow students to relearn or explain their error in thinking.
Task Analysis	Determine specific steps students must master to complete a task. Some students can be graded on each step they completed versus being assessed on the entire task assigned.
Diagnostic Probes and Diagnostic Teaching	Use short, one-minute review pages reinforce critical skills. One teacher makes a probe to summarize the critical skills each week and then begins each class each day with various 1-3 minute probes.
Checklists and Rating Scales (see Exhibit 7.7)	Ask students to complete a self-reflection on their skills in a particular area, or use these tools to check off or rate a student's ability on each step of a task. This tool can be used with a task analysis, or a class-wide checklist can be created and then used in a modified format for students with more involved academic or behavioral needs. This checklist can be used for students to compare their behavior or skills to an average student in the class.
Questionnaires, Interviews and Focus Groups	Provide students with questionnaires about the school and how effectively teachers are meeting their needs. Also, conduct focus groups to determine how teaching impacts students' perceptions and learning.
Evaluating the Learning Environment	Assess changes needed in the learning environment. Many schools choose to have some consistency in the way the environment is developed (e.g., same rules in all classrooms, students working in cooperative groups). As you are assessing student performance, also assess the environment they are in throughout the day (e.g., noise levels, seat height).
Exhibitions	Use this tool to help students select how they will demonstrate mastery of a concept and exhibit their skills to teachers, peers, parents, and community members. This type of assessment is typically paired with a rubric to assist in evaluating the learning.

Exhibit 7.6 ~ Work Sample

WORK SAMPLE DESCRIPTION

NAME: _____ SUBJECT: _____

DATE: _____ DOMAIN: _____

ACCURACY: [_____ %]   STRAND: _____

INDEPENDENCE: [_____ %]   STANDARD: _____

BENCHMARK: _____

TARGETED SKILL: _____
_____
_____

BRIEF DESCRIPTION OF THE ACTIVITY: _____
_____
_____

Table created by Christine Ogilvie, used with written permission – Copyright 2006

Exhibit 7.7 ~ End of the Day Checklist

End of Day Checklist   Date: _____

Did I ... ?

_____   ... go to my locker as soon as I came into school?

_____   ... organize my materials for my classes?

_____   ... give my home folder to my teacher?

_____   ... review my homework with a teacher?

_____   ... get a blank homework sheet from my teacher?

_____   ... bring all necessary materials with me to class?

_____   ... write down all my homework for all classes?

_____   ... use my free time to work on homework?

_____   ... demonstrate appropriate coping skills in stressful situations?

            _____   ... take a step back and think about the situation?

            _____   ... ask a friend or adult for help?

_____   ... respond appropriately to direct questions?

            _____   ... stay focused?

            _____   ... answer what was being asked?

Total # of checks: _____   _____
                                            (signature)

_____
(teacher signature)

Table created by Christine Ogilvie used with written permission – Copyright 2006

There will probably always be traditional paper and pencil assessments that students will have to complete. Again, in the perfect world, there would be plenty of time to modify tests. But, in the real world, we may have to modify the assessment tool as we enter the classroom. As mentioned in earlier chapters on collaboration, to make our jobs easier, we need to share our work. At the secondary level, I have found much redundancy. For example, in one situation, all four special educators modified the same test in a different way. In a strong collaborative and inclusive school, materials would be shared and there would be a resource center where modified/adapted materials are kept for use by all teachers so that there is minimal duplication of efforts. In order to address this issue of modifying materials, Janet Hill, an excellent classroom teacher and colleague, developed quick and easy suggestions for modifying the tests or grading structure, instead of always focusing on extending time. A summary of these follows:

Informal Adaptation/Modification of Assessment tools
Before the Test
- Identify concept maps, study guides, graphic organizers and allow students to use these on the test.
- Provide pre-made note cards of key points to study.
- Provide practice tests that students can review at home.
- Offer individual/group review before or after school.
- Teach test taking strategies.
- Teach mnemonics.
- Chunk material into groups so that the brain can process.

During the Test
- Check Anxiety Level — Ask students before the test how they feel about the test and provide support to those who don't feel positive.
- Give Immediate Feedback — If students get the first question right, tell them!
- Complete one problem/question from each section with the entire class.
- Provide an alternative site — but remember we recall items best in the places we learned them, so only move students out of the classroom if needed for attention or extended time.
- Teach self-monitoring – show students how to monitor where they should be at what time point.

- Provide extended time – but remember that the student may be mentally exhausted and additional time is not always the answer.

After the Test
- Allow students to retake the test.
- Allow students to make corrections or to verbally tell you the errors of their ways for half credit.
- Use an alternative type of grading structure: The suggestions provided are based on a traditional 30 question test. Here are some alternative ways of grading/modifying the test without having to create a new test:
  - 30 questions — The test is worth 25 points, but the student is allowed to try all 30 questions so that getting 25 correct would allow the student to have a grade of 100% correct.
  - 30 questions — Teacher grades only those twenty items identified with a star as important for mastery of topic or reflecting the Power Standards.
  - 30 questions — Student attempts twenty three of the total questions in the time allotted and misses three. The grade is calculated as a percentage using twenty out of twenty three questions, or 86.9%.
  - Multiple Grades — Instead of only giving one grade for the 30 question test, consider a grade for the content and another grade for mechanics.
  - Give Partial Credit — Tell students that any attempt at the question will earn them partial credit; this makes students more willing to try all questions, even ones they may not be certain they know.

Test Anxiety
For many students, tests present a tremendous challenge, not just because of the material that must be mastered but often due to their reaction to the test taking situation itself. This challenge is not just for students with disabilities, but can impact any student. The result frequently is that students are not able to adequately demonstrate what they know because anxiety depresses their ability to respond. This phenomenon of test anxiety has increased due to the focus placed on higher standards and test

scores. In attempts to raise achievement, anxiety is also raised, with depressed scores as the result. Therefore, it is very important that teachers and parents not only understand the cause and symptoms of test anxiety, but also that they are armed with strategies and techniques to reduce its negative effects. An excellent book that addresses this topic is *Test Anxiety & What You Can Do About It,* Casbarro (2005).

Test Construction

Another reason students with disabilities sometimes receive failing grades is because of the way tests are constructed. I have provided some guidelines and suggestions for how to make various types of tests more accessible and helpful for students with disabilities.

Matching Items

Try to use the same number of items in each column and keep the list to seven to ten items. Put the items in the same order that they were taught in class. Try to keep all items on the same page so that students do not have to flip back and forth to find the answers.

Multiple Choice

Always use simple sentences for both the questions posed and the choice of responses. Consider even having students write questions that you use on the test and put the students' names next to the questions they authored. Limit the number of choices to no more than 4 and less even if the student has a more significant disability. Always list items vertically and not horizontally.

Sentence Completion

Provide students with visual cues or give them the first letter of the correct response. This type of cue can help prompt students' memory. Try not to use complex or tricky sentences. Offer students a word bank to assist them in selecting the correct response.

True/False

Try to use simple sentences and stay away from tricky words or responses. Try not to have more than seven to ten questions that are true/false on a test, and always avoid the use of double negatives.

Essay and short answer

Allow students to use the semantic maps or graphic organizers they created on the test. Provide some visual cues, work lists, or even phrases to assist students in covering the key points. When creating the question, be very clear as to the number of points you want students to provide (e.g., provide three reasons why…). Use simple sentences and be prepared to either read the question to a student, or have the question available on tape for the student to listen to on a tape recorder at their desk. If needed, allow the student to use a scribe to answer (this can be done into a video recorder if a scribe is not available), or type their response on an Alphasmart or computer.

Creating tools that allow students to learn from the teachers' perspective is important. Yet, even more important is the skill of self-advocacy mentioned in Chapter 2 that ensures students know their strengths, embrace their weakness, and advocate for themselves when their needs are not being met.

No matter how we assess students with disabilities, they may not be successful if we continue to use a single method to measure performance. By moving away from traditional paper/pencil assessments to a more diverse assessment system that evaluates students using a variety of methods, we can begin to clearly understand what students do and do not know. Assessment systems need to go beyond just factual information and embrace what the field of special education has been focusing on since its inception as a field — success in life. Finally, students need to be taught about how they learn best and, equally important, how they can most effectively exhibit the knowledge they have acquired. We will have arrived as an educational system when a student's inability to see, speak, read, write, hear or walk is recognized not by the failing of traditional assessments, but by success in schools that create unique environments for learning and assessment, and celebrate their abilities. The expectation in inclusive schools is that students' diverse needs will be considered in all assessments and their unique ways of learning will be measured with tools that celebrate their individuality. Learning is about student success, and learning cannot be measured by one single moment in time or with one single tool. In a truly inclusive environment, the toolbox of assessment instruments and creative ways students can demonstrate learning must be as diverse as the students served.

Reflective Questions

1. How do our current grading systems celebrate the diversity of students in our school or classroom?
2. Which additional grading systems would work for our classroom?
3. How would we need to change or modify our current grading system to facilitate an inclusive classroom?
4. What are our beliefs about grading, class participation and evaluating learning?

References

Balfanz, R. & Legters, N. (2004). *Locating the dropout crisis: Which high schools produce the nation's dropouts? Where are they located? Who attends them?* Center for Research on the Education of Students Place At Risk Report 70: John Hopkins University.

Casbarro, Joseph. (2005). *Test Anxiety & What You Can Do About*
It. Port Chester, NY: Dude Publishing.

Keefe, E. B., Moore, V., & Duff, F. (2004). The four "knows" of collaborative teaching. *Teaching Exceptional Children, 36*(5), 36-42.

Laframboise, K. L., Epanchin, B., Colucci, K., & Hocutt, A. (2004). Working together: Emerging roles of special and general education teachers in inclusive settings. *Action in Teacher Education, 26*(3), 29-43.

Munk, D. (2003). *Solving the grading puzzle.* Whitefish Bay, WI: Knowledge by Design.

Obiakor, F. E., Obi, S. O., & Algozzine, B. (2001). Shifting assessment and intervention paradigms for urban learners. *The Western Journal of Black Studies, 25*(1), 61-71.

Salend, S. J. (2002). Grading students in inclusive settings. *Teaching Exceptional Children, 34*(3), 8-15.

Stecker, P. M., & Fuchs, L. S. (2000). Effecting superior achievement using curriculum-based measurement: The importance of individual progress monitoring. *Learning Disabilities*

Research & Practice, 15(3), 128-134.

Voltz, D. L., Sims, M. J., Nelson, B., & Bivens, C. (2005). A framework for inclusion in the context of standards-based reform. *Teaching Exceptional Children, 37*(5), 14-19.

Walsh, D., & Matlock, L. (2000). Demonstrating achievement in special education. *Thrust for Educational Leadership, 29*(4), 34-36.

Chapter **8**

Where To Go From Here

There is a saying that change comes slowly, but that it does not matter how slow the process as long as it does not stop! This statement may be appropriate when talking about change in business practices or in creating a better car, but the same statement is troubling related to the education and lives of children. Research indicates that schools take three to five years to adopt new and best/promising practices. Yet, consider that any student who is currently a freshman will probably no longer be at the school in five years to receive any benefit from the change. By the time change occurs, the disabled student could be yet another drop-out statistic. In response to change, however, I have seen positive learning outcomes and a shared sense of success when students with disabilities are included in the general education setting. In these successful schools, teachers act differently but, more importantly, students who are different feel a sense of sameness by being given the opportunity to have the same teachers, sit at the same desks, and learn the same "good stuff" as their non-disabled peers.

American schools were created with a promise of providing an education for all students. Viable universal education in this country will exist when all students are accepted by teachers at all levels. Inclusion is not just an elementary initiative, but is expected across all grade levels in every district, ensuring that all students share in that promise, that is known to have both social and economic impact on students' lives.

In pursuit of this promise, the final chapter of this book provides several tools that can be used to develop and/or refine a stronger and more inclusive secondary education for all students, including those with disabilities.

One of my favorite activities, and one that has been very well received, is *The Perfect School,* as seen in Exhibit 8.1. In this activity I ask teams of teachers and administrators to dream about what their staff, resources, schools, classrooms, and community would look like if they had endless fiscal resources. I find this activity encourages staff to talk positively, and to think about what might be, instead of what is not. Often, at the secondary level, staff is so mired in the status quo that it takes an activity like this to help them think outside the day to day life of the school. This activity is also a great way to remind teachers that dreaming is a necessary component of change. Often, while thinking about what will work in these schools, teachers talk about having items such as a copy machine that works, or faster access to printers. I quickly redirect them to dream big: Why not have a secretary for teachers, high-speed, color copy machine, or a scanner that transmits all materials directly to students' laptops on their desks. Teachers quickly begin to add their own great ideas, such as a personal trainer for each teacher, a five-star chef to cook meals, and even a jet plane to fly students to fieldtrips across the globe. Throughout this activity teachers are filled with laughter and smiles. Inevitably though, what occurs is that teachers identify some items that they realize they could actually have, such as classrooms that are closer together so teachers can collaborate more easily, or greater access to computers for all students.

After ten minutes of dreaming and sharing the most grandiose ideas, the groups are then challenged to come up with at least one idea related to inclusive education that they will make a reality in their school. Then, in a matter of five to ten minutes, each group typically identifies a potential action item they could implement in their school, based upon being given permission to think outside the traditional constraints of the status quo. The activity is not just about inclusion, but also about laughter, dreaming, and celebrating the power teachers have to make change happen. Schools that are inclusive realize that "together we are better," and that their strength lies in the entire learning community — staff, students, and families — feeling empowered to make their school the best learning environment possible.

Exhibit 8.1 ~ The Perfect School

If you had all the fiscal resources in the world, what would your "perfect school" look like, sound like, feel like, and/or be like?

Staff

      Administration

      Teachers

      Support Staff

Resources

      Building

      Materials

Community

      Parents

      Business

      Agencies

      Other

Another activity I recommend is called *Celebrating Staff Strengths,* as seen in Exhibit 8.2. At a staff meeting, teachers are asked to list two things they do well and that they are willing to share. Staff need to be reminded not to focus on things such as baking chocolate chip cookies or having a great golf swing, but instead must select professional skills they would like to celebrate and share.

What does this activity have to do with inclusive schools? Once complete, this list of strengths is posted in the teachers' lounge and used to foster greater collaboration. For example, if an in-service presentation is needed in a specific area and a staff member acknowledges this as a strength, rather than bringing in an outside person, let this teacher present or share their skills. This list also is invaluable to new teachers. They can review this list and ask for support and advice in any areas in which they feel help would be significant. Building a system for stronger collaboration among teachers is difficult, especially in large middle and high schools, yet it is critical for staff to collaborate in strong inclusive schools.

This same list can also be used to identify areas in need of further support or professional development/staff training in the school. For example, if no one in the school lists cooperative learning as an area of strength, then this might be considered a target for professional development. However, instead of bringing in someone to do a workshop on cooperative learning, a more effective model might be to identify another school or district that is using this model and arrange a visit to observe this practice in action. After a visit to a school that uses true cooperative learning, ask an administrator to arrange for teachers from the visitation site to come in and provide coaching on this technique. This coaching may lead to the development of peer relationships that can be utilized over a period of time.

Just as children need to be celebrated for their strengths, so do teachers. Listing strenghts therefore becomes a springboard for professional celebrations. I have yet to be in a secondary school where students come running in the door, telling their teachers how grateful they are for all that the teacher does to ensure their learning! Schools that celebrate the strengths of their students through inclusive practices also celebrate the teachers who take ownership everyday of the important task of guiding student learning.

Exhibit 8.2 ~ Celebrating Staff Strengths

Next to your name below, write two skills you have that you would be willing to share with other teachers.

Name	Strength	Strength

Dieker, 2006.

At the end of each chapter of this book, there is a series of reflective questions related to the topics covered. In this chapter, the questions are being included earlier, as they provide a framework for eliciting thoughts, feelings, and ideas related to inclusive practices. Teachers can use these questions to talk about schoolwide changes and classroom changes that might improve the learning of all students, with a focus on students with disabilities. Responses to these questions can also be used in the final activity of the chapter.

1. At this time, what do you see as your school's greatest strengths?
2. What contributions do you see yourself making to your school's current success(es)?
3. What are two areas that you feel still need to be improved within your school related to inclusion?
4. What suggestions do you have for improving these areas?
5. What power do you see yourself having in making changes to improve your school?
6. What one thing will you do within the next week to begin to make these changes happen?

Exhibit 8.3 is another instrument for data collection. It is a worksheet that frames questions around the topical areas of this book. Thus, it provides a review as well as a summary. It can be used in a variety of ways, such as listed below.

1. Use this checklist for self-reflection on classroom instruction or school performance related to inclusion.
2. Use this checklist with a co-teaching colleague to determine where changes may need to occur at the classroom level and what barriers might exists at the school-wide level related to inclusive practices.
3. Use this tool to educate others about the components that are present in strong inclusive schools.
4. Use this tool with the entire staff to determine what is working and to determine areas in need of further improvement to create a plan as to how to effectively address the needs of students with disabilities.

Exhibit 8.3 ~ School-wide and Classroom Based Teacher Expectations/ Behaviors In Successful Inclusive Schools

Question to frame your responses: Are students with disabilities not ready for the general education setting, or is the general education setting not ready for the learning and/or behavioral needs of students with disabilities?

7 Effective School-Wide Strategies Worksheet

Strategy	Strength(s) in this area	School goal for this area	Personal goal for this area
Creating a School-Wide Culture for Inclusion			
Celebrating the Success of All Students			
Developing Interdisciplinary Collaboration			
Implementing Effective Co-Teaching			
Establishing Active Learning Environments			
Implementing Successful Instruction			
Improving Grading and Student Assessment			

7 Effective Classroom Instruction Behaviors

Strategy	Strength(s) in this area	School goal for this area	Personal goal for this area
Prior to the start of each quarter teachers discuss: curricular goals, IEP goals, behavior management, grading and assessment for students with disabilities.			
Students with disabilities are given as many opportunities to give to others as they are to receive help.			
Classroom materials are rich and diverse, and include material embraced by "info-kids."			
Lesson Presentation: a) teacher talk is less than 50% of the lesson, b) teacher talk is paired with visuals, c) social skills are part of the lesson, and d) learning is active.			
Physical breaks occur at least once a period but ideally every 8-10 mins.			
Knowledge is presented in chunks.			
Multiple ways exist to assess students beyond paper and pencil tests.			

How do ideas, suggestions, strategies, and theories become reality? All the thinking in the world won't accomplish anything unless there is a plan that supports and structures the change. Therefore, through Exhibit 8.4, staff is encouraged to work together to develop an action plan for addressing the areas for change identified throughout this book. I typically start this activity by asking the questions, "If, in 10 years, someone were to walk into your school, how would they know it was an inclusive school? What would they see or hear that convinced them that all children are celebrated and belong in the general education setting?" The responses to these questions provide a perfect opportunity to discuss the need for, and value of, a clear plan that enunciates a long-range vision. This plan becomes a legacy for the next generation of teachers and leaders who are committed to inclusive education.

The process in Exhibit 8.4 can be used when schools are trying to make systemic change. I suggest that schools start their planning by creating a visual image of all classrooms in their school, and noting where students with disabilities are currently being served. I then recommend that staff list all supports available within the school and how these supports might be used in creating an inclusive climate. I typically end the activity by asking schools to identify five year, three year and one year goals related to the initial ten year vision created by the team. I then ask that each teacher in the school take ownership for one action item that will foster change.

Exhibit 8.4 ~ Action Plan

Now that you have envisioned the perfect school, identified the strengths of your school, and targeted areas in need of improvement, it is time to develop an action plan to start moving towards making your school "The Perfect School" in relation to serving students with disabilities.

1. Draw a diagram of all of the classrooms in your school.

2. Star those that already include students with disabilities.

3. List supports that are currently provided in those classrooms, as well as all other resources that are available in your school.

4. Circle those teachers who currently do not have students included but would be willing to move in this direction.

5. Decide how to best expand the inclusion of students with disabilities in your school.
   Family model — Should teams of teachers be empowered to design their own models for meeting students' needs?
   Co-teaching — Should special educators be aligned either by caseload or by content to provide support through co-teaching?
   Support Teacher — Are there classes that need only short-term support or where peer mentors could be put into the classroom instead of a full-time special education teacher?
   Itinerant Teacher — Are there classes that the special educator needs to rotate through one day a week to provide moderate support, depending on the level of students' functioning?

6. Discuss target groups/students for these classrooms.

7. How will you build a positive climate?

8. Will you need to adapt the curriculum?

9. Will you need to adapt instruction?

10. Develop a reflective framework to evaluate your implementation plan.

I wish everyone who reads this book all of the energy, knowledge, and heart that is so desperately needed to change our secondary schools. My hope is that these changes will focus not on meeting standards, or regulations, but instead on meeting the needs of every child, adolescent, and human being that walks through the doors of school to provide them what they need to succeed not in school — but in *life*.

> *Thank you for taking the time to think about how we can ensure that all students' voices are heard, and for being the voice for those who cannot or are not allowed to speak for themselves. Happy inclusion.*
>
> — Lisa Dieker

Appendix A ~ Adolescent Literature

As introduced in Chapter 5, this compilation of adolescent literature that focuses on various topics related to disabilities. It can be used in a variety of ways. Although developed initially by Juanita William, a secondary English teacher, to help students learn more about differences of people with disabilities, it is also an excellent resource for the development of general library resources within a secondary school.

Title	Author	Summary from the World Wide Web	Category	Ms. William's Reflections
Shell Lady's Daughter (The)	Adler, C.S.	When fourteen-year-old Kelly is sent off to Florida to stay with her rigid grandparents after her mother's nervous breakdown, she learns the meaning of love and support.	Mental Illness	Kelly's mom overdoses on sleeping pills and goes into inpatient psych treatment for depression. Since Kelly's dad is a pilot, she has to go stay with a dragonesque grandmother in Palm Beach. Parent of main character has serious depression.
Do You Remember the Color Blue?: and other questions kids ask about blindness	Alexander, Sally Hobart	Children ask questions of an author who lost her vision at the age of twenty-seven, including "How did you become blind?" "How can you read?" and "Was it hard to be a parent when you couldn't see your kids?"	Blind	I really like this book. The pictures are out of date but the writing is clear and direct. Main character is blind.
Tangerine	Bloor, Edward	Twelve-year-old Paul, who lives in the shadow of his football hero brother Erik, fights for the right to play soccer despite his near blindness and slowly begins to remember the incident that damaged his eyesight.	Visually Handicapped/ Physically Handicapped	This book just didn't grab me. The main character has severe visual impairment and is an amazing soccer player.

Title	Author	Topic	Description
Sahara Special	Codell, Esmé Raji	Teacher-student relationships	Struggling with school and her feelings of loss since her father left, Sahara gets a fresh start with a new and unique teacher who supports her writing talents and the individuality of each of her classmates.	This is a lovely book that speaks to the teacher in me. It's more about understanding children who don't trust teachers than it is about disabilities, but there are important themes of the sometimes stigma of being a special needs kid and trying to fit in a regular world when you're struggling and/or different. Main character is failing in school and trying to make it in regular classes.
St. Michael's Scales	Connelly, Neil	Mental Illness	Keegan Flannery, feeling responsible for his twin brother's death and his mother's mental illness, believes he must atone by committing suicide before his sixteenth birthday, but he gains new insights when he joins his school's wrestling team.	Keegan is deeply depressed and hears his dead twin brother's voice. Somehow, no one sees this issue or tries to help this kid. He mystically works through things on his own and in the end saves his own life. I don't care for the themes of don't trust parents or counselors, and teens can work out these major issues on their own. Main character has depression and possibly other psychoses, his mom is hospitalized after a nervous breakdown.
Whale Talk	Crutcher, Chris	Mental Disabilities	Intellectually and athletically gifted, TJ, a multiracial, adopted teenager, shuns organized sports and the gung-ho athletes at his high school until he agrees to form a swimming team and recruits some of the school's less popular students.	I love this book! One of the main characters is a young man who was brain damaged as a result of child abuse. He discovers a talent for swimming and an unusual team changes his life. One character with brain damage and one with a missing leg.

Title	Author	Summary	Category	Comment
Of Sound Mind	Ferris, Jean	Tired of interpreting for his deaf family and resentful of their reliance on him, high school senior Theo finds support and understanding from Ivy, a new student who also has a deaf parent.	Deaf/Physically Handicapped	This is an incredible book!! Jean Ferris is such a great writer. Wow!! The parents and brother of the main character are deaf and his girlfriend's father is deaf, too.
Joey Pigza Loses Control	Gantos, Jack	Joey, who is still taking medication to keep him from getting too wired, goes to spend the summer with the hard-drinking father he has never known and tries to help the baseball team he coaches win the championship.	ADHD	I didn't enjoy the sequel as much as the original, but the character of Joey is as engaging as ever. The main character has ADHD.
Joey Pigza Swallowed the Key	Gantos, Jack	To the constant disappointment of his mother and teachers, Joey has trouble paying attention or controlling his mood swings when his prescription meds wear off and he starts getting worked up and acting wired.	ADHD	You just have to love Joey Pigza! The descriptions of how it feels to have a mind and body "loaded with springs" are well worth the read. The main character has ADHD.
What Would Joey Do?	Gantos, Jack	Joey tries to keep his life from degenerating into total chaos when his mother sends him to be home-schooled with a hostile blind girl, his divorced parents cannot stop fighting, and his grandmother is dying of emphysema.	Blind/ADHD	Third Joey Pigza book. Please refer to the other comments. The main character has ADHD.
The Curious Incident of the Dog in the Night-time	Haddon, Mark	Despite his overwhelming fear of interacting with people, Christopher, a mathematically-gifted, autistic fifteen-year-old boy, decides to investigate the murder of a neighbor's dog and uncovers secret information about his mother.	Autism - fiction	I like this story and feel that it holds up to multiple readings. Some of the language isn't middle school appropriate. The main character is high-functioning autistic.

Title	Author	Summary	Category	Review
One Child	Hayden, Torey L.	Six-year-old Sheila never spoke, never cried, and her eyes were filled with hate. Abandoned on a highway by her mother, abused by her alcoholic father, Sheila was placed in a class for the hopelessly retarded after she committed an atrocious act of violence against another child.	Child Abuse Child Psychopath	This book is a real gut-wrencher. All future teachers, especially special educaiton teachers, should read this one. Sheila makes you want to scoop her up and bring her home. The main character is assumed to be pro-foundly retarded but is, in fact, a genius.
Kissing Doorknobs	Hesser, Terry Spencer	Fourteen-year-old Tara describes how her increasingly strange compulsions begin to take over her life and affect her relation-ships with her family and friends.	Mental Illness/Obsessive-Compulsive Disorder	This book is really a good read. The frustration and anger that Tara feels over her strange behaviors is clearly written and you just feel for this girl and her family. Main character is a girl with obsessive compulsive disorder.
Stoner & Spaz	Koertge, Ron	A troubled youth with cerebral palsy struggles toward self-acceptance with the help of a drug-addicted young woman.	Cerebral Palsy	This book has a positive ending but doesn't wrap up all of the endings in a tidy little bow. Gritty and real (translate that to some nonexplicit sex and drugs).Main character has cerebral palsy.
The Silent Boy	Lowry, Lois	Katy, the precocious ten-year-old daughter of the town doctor, befriends a boy who is mentally retarded.	Mental Disabilities	This is a good example of photo inspired writing. Perhaps a good kick-off book for beginning a unit on mental disabilities and the history of their treatment. Not my personal favorite read. Some of the story action centers around a boy with mental retardation.

Title	Author	Description	Category	Comments
Pictures in the Dark	McCord, Patricia	Life with their mother who is mentally ill becomes unbearable for twelve-year-old Sarah and fifteen-year-old Carlie as they are deprived of food and forbidden to use the bathroom.	Mental Illness	The girls live in constant fear of their unbalanced mother. When they finally get the courage to speak up things begin to get better. This is a tough book to read. Main character's mother has a nervous breakdown.
Sparks	McNamee, Graham	When Todd is both happy and anxious about trying to fit in with the regular fifth grade class but feels confused about how to relate to his former friends in the Special Needs class, a school assignment on the exploited pygmy, Ota Benga, helps give him confidence and clarity.	Learning Disabilities	This is a great story of leaving Special Education and trying to fit into regular classes. The main character is trying so hard to fit in and succeed that he almost loses his best friend from Special Education. The main character has a learning disability.
Keep Stompin' till the Music Stops	Pevsner, Stella	Twelve-year-old Richard struggles to achieve independence in spite of a learning disability while his great-grandfather defies the family's plans to curtail his own independent lifestyle.	Learning Disabilities	Richard is singled out for extra work all summer and is embarrassed by his parents at a family reunion. His good relationship with a cousin helps him get through all this family togetherness. The main character has a learning disability.
Freak the Mighty	Philbrick, Rodman	At the beginning of eighth grade, Max, who is learning disabled, and his new friend Freak, whose birth defect has affected his body but not his brilliant mind, find that when they combine forces they make a powerful team.	Learning Disabilities/ Physically Handicapped	A boy with LD and a mini-wizard with serious health issues form a team with sizzling synergy! I loved this book and can't wait to see the movie. Main characters are a boy with LD and a boy who is physically disabled.

Title	Author	Description	Category	Review
Matthew Unstrung	Seago, Kate	A 17-year-old boy who suffered a mental breakdown in the early 1900s is able to regain his sanity with the help of his brother.	Mental Illness	This is a good period piece with pretty upsetting images of how the mentally ill were treated in asylums in the early 1900s. Great story of redemption between caring family members. Main character has a nervous breakdown and is nursed to health by his brother.
Pay Attention, Slosh!	Smith, Mark	Eight-year-old Josh hates being unable to concentrate or control himself, but with the help of his parents, his teacher, and a doctor, he learns to deal with his condition, known as ADHD or attention-deficit hyperactivity disorder.	Learning Disabilities/ ADHD	This is a third or fourth grade reading level book about Josh's diagnosis of, and treatment for, ADHD. Main character is a child with ADHD.
Looking for Jamie Bridger	Springer, Nancy	Fourteen-year-old Jamie Bridger is determined to find out who her real parents were in spite of opposition from the grandparents who raised her, but her search ends in a bittersweet discovery.	Mental Illness	Fabulous book! Weirdly strange and wonderful. It's hard to talk about it without giving too much away but I would never have guessed the ending and I love that. Main character's family (Gramma and Grandpa) have mental illness.
Tru Confessions	Tashjian, Janet	Computer-literate, twelve-year-old Tru keeps an electronic diary where she documents her desire to cure her twin brother, who is disabled, and her plan to create a television show.	Mental Disabilities	Awesome! This book had me grinning and tearing up all the way through. A must read for children dealing with a sibling with special needs. One of the main characters is a child with mental retardation.

Title	Author	Description	Disability	Notes
Multiple Choice	Tashjian, Janet	Monica, a fourteen-year-old perfectionist and word game expert, tries to break free from all of the suffocating rules in her life by creating a game for living called Multiple Choice.	Mental Illness/Obsessive-Compulsive Disorder	I really like Monica. She tries so hard to overcome her issues. The choices she creates for her Multiple Choice game are mostly funny until they get scary. Main character is a girl with obsessive/compulsive disorder.
Cruise Control	Trueman, Terry	A talented basketball player struggles to deal with the helplessness and anger that come with having a brother rendered completely dysfunctional by severe cerebral palsy and a father who deserted the family.	Cerebral Palsy	This is a companion book to *Stuck in Neutral* and narrates some of the same events from the perspective of the older brother who invests his life in sports to deal with the pain of his family trauma. Brother of main character has severe CP.
Inside Out	Trueman, Terry	A sixteen-year-old with schizophrenia is caught up in the events surrounding an attempted robbery by two other teens that eventually hold him hostage.	Schizophrenia/Mental Illness	This is a short and quite compelling story. The story cuts back and forth between the hostage situation and descriptions of the voices in Zach's head. A really interesting look at schizophrenia. The main character is a boy with paranoid schizophrenia.
Stuck in Neutral	Trueman, Terry	Fourteen-year-old Shawn McDaniel, who suffers from severe cerebral palsy and cannot function, relates his perceptions of his life, his family, and his condition, especially as he believes his father is planning to kill him.	Cerebral Palsy	The main character has no muscle control of any part of his body and no means to communicate but is smart and witty on the inside. His seizures free him to spirit walk around Seattle and are his favorite part of his life. Very intense story of how this disability affects his family. Main character has severe CP.

Title	Author	Category	Summary	Notes
How to be a Real Person (in just one day)	Warner, Sally	Mental Illness	Sixth grader Kara tries to conceal from her friends, her absent father, and the authorities that her mother is sliding deeper and deeper into mental illness.	This is a sweet and sad book. Kara's connection with the book *Island of the Blue Dolphins* offers a potential classroom tie-in. This reminds me again how tough it is for some children to come to school and behave normally when their home life is in chaos. The mother of the main character is mentally ill.
So B. It: A Novel	Weeks, Sarah	Mental Illness	After spending her life with her mother, who is mentally disabled, and neighbor, who is agoraphobic, twelve-year-old Heidi sets out from Reno, Nevada, to New York to find out who she is.	One of my favorite things from this book is Heidi's luck. She's 12 and lives with her mom and a neighbor but has never been to school or the movies or anywhere besides a few stores and her apartment. Heidi is a great kid. Main character's mother is mentally disabled (only speaks 23 words) and her neighbor (who is like a second mom) is agoraphobic.
Memories of Summer	White, Ruth	Mental Illness	In 1955, thirteen-year-old Lyric finds her whole life changing when her family moves from the hills of Virginia to a town in Michigan and her older sister Summer begins descending into mental illness.	Lyric and her father work so hard to try and keep Summer at home but she becomes dangerous to herself and others. Lyric ends up with only memories of her close relationship with Summer. Main character's sister has schizophrenia.
Naked without a hat	Willis, Jeanne	Down Syndrome People with mental disabilities	Promising to keep his mother's secret, eighteen-year-old Will moves into a house for people with disabilities, falls in love with a young Gypsy woman, and learns to assert his own identity and independence.	I like this British story. It's told from the perspective of a young man with Down Syndrome who finally gets to live on his own and falls in love. Some of the language isn't school appropriate. Several of the characters are young men with mental disabilities.

Written permission from Juanita Williams, 2006

Resources: Print and Video Materials
Available from National Professional Resources, Inc.
1-800 453-7461 • www.NPRinc.com

Allington, Richard L. & Patricia M. Cunningham. *Schools That Work: Where all Children Read and Write.* New York, NY: Harper Collins, 1996.

Aranha, Mary. *A Good Place To Be: A Leadership Guide for Making Your Vision a Reality…Within Your School, Within Your Classroom, Within Your Family, Within Your Heart.* Port Chester, NY: Dude Publishing, 2002.

Armstrong, Thomas. *Beyond the ADD Myth: Classroom Strategies & Techniques* (Video). Port Chester, NY: National Professional Resources, Inc, 1996.

Armstrong, Thomas. *The Myth of the A.D.D. Child.* New York, NY: Penguin Putnam Inc., 1997.

ASCD. *How to Co-teach to Meet Diverse Students Needs* (Video). Baltimore, MD: ASCD, 2006.

ASCD. Teaching Students with Learning Disabilities in the Regular Classroom (Video). Baltimore, MD: ASCD, 2006.

Basso, Dianne, & Natalie McCoy. The Co-Teaching Manual. Columia, SC: Twin Publications, 2002.

Bateman, Barbara D. & Annemieke Golly. *Why Johnny Doesn't Behave: Twenty Tips for Measurable BIPs.* Verona, WI: Attainment Company, Inc., 2003.

Bateman, Barbara D. & Cynthia M. Herr. *Writing Measurable IEP Goals and Objectives.* Verona, WI: Attainment Company, Inc., 2003.

Batshaw, Mark L. *Children with Disabilities, 5th Edition.* Baltimore, MD: Paul H. Brookes Publishing, 2002.

Bauer, Anne & Glenda Brown. *Adolescents and Inclusion: Transforming Secondary Schools.* Baltimore, MD: Brookes Publishing Company, 2001.

Beattie, John, LuAnn Jordan, & Bob Algozzine. *Making Inclusion Work.* Thousand Oaks, CA: Corwin Publishing, 2006.

Beecher, Margaret. *Developing the Gifts & Talents of All Students in the Regular Classroom.* Mansfield Center, CT: Creative Learning Press, Inc., 1995.

Bender, William. *Differentiating Instruction for Students with Learning Disabilities.* Thousand Oaks, CA: Corwin Press, 2002.

Bocchino, Rob. *Emotional Literacy: To Be a Different Kind of Smart.* Thousand Oaks, CA: Corwin Press, 1999.

Brady, Kathryn, Mary Beth Forton, Deborah Porter, & Chip Wood. *Rules in School.* Turners Falls, MA: Northeast Foundation for Children, 2003.

Bray, Marty & Abbie Brown, et al. *Technology and the Diverse Learner.* Thousand Oaks, CA: Corwin Press, 2004.

Brown-Chidsey, Rachel & Mark W. Steege. *Response to Intervention.* New York, NY: Guilford Press, 2005.

Buehler, Bruce. *What We Know…How We Teach – Linking Medicine & Education for the Child with Special Needs* (Video). Port Chester, NY: National Professional Resources, Inc., 1998.

Bunch, Gary. *Inclusion: How To.* Toronto, Canada: Inclusion Press, 1999.

Burrello, Leonard, Carol Lashly, & Edith E. Beaty. *Educating All Students Together: How School Leaders Create Unified Systems.* Thousand Oaks, CA: Corwin Press, Inc., 2001.

Casbarro, Joseph. *Test Anxiety & What You Can Do About It: A Practical Guide for Teachers, Parents, & Kids.* Port Chester, NY: Dude Publishing, 2005.

Chapman, Carolyn & Rita King. *Differentiated Instructional Strategies for Reading in the Content Areas.* Thousand Oaks, CA: Corwin Press, 2003.

Cohen, Jonathan. *Educating Minds and Hearts: Social Emotional Learning and the Passage into Adolescence.* New York, NY: Teachers College Press, 1999.

Connor, Daniel F. *Aggression and Antisocial Behavior in Children and Adolescents: Research and Treatment.* New York, NY: The Guilford Press, 2004.

Courtade-Little, Ginevra, & Diane M. Browder. *Aligning IEPs to Academic Standards: For Students with Moderate and Severe Disabilities.* Verona, WI: Attainment Company, Inc., 2005.

Council for Exceptional Children and Merrill Education. *Universal Design for Learning.* Atlanta, GA: 2005.

Crawford, Glenda B. *Managing the Adolescent Classroom.* Thousand Oaks, CA: Corwin Press, 2004.

Crone, Deanne A. & Robert H. Horner. *Building Positive Behavior Support Systems in Schools: Functional Behavioral Assessment.* New York, NY: Guilford Press, 2003.

Darling-Hammond, Linda. *The New Teacher: Meeting the Challenges* (Video). Port Chester, NY: National Professional Resources, Inc., 2000.

Deiner, Penny Low. *Resources for Educating Children with Diverse Abilities, 4th Edition.* Florence, KY: Thomson Delmar Learning, 2004.

Deshler, Donald D. & Jean B. Schumaker. *Teaching Adolescents With Disabilities: Accessing the General Education Curriculum.* Thousand Oaks, CA: Corwin Press, 2005.

Dieker, Lisa. *7 Effective Strategies for Secondary Inclusion (Video).* Port Chester, NY: National Professional Resources, Inc., 2006.

Dieker, Lisa. *Co-Teaching Lesson Plan Book (Third Edition).* Whitefish Bay, WI: Knowledge By Design, 2006.

Dodge, Judith. *Differentiation in Action.* Jefferson City, MO: Scholastic Inc., 2005.

Dover, Wendy. *Inclusion: The Next Step* (3-ring binder). Manhattan, KS: MASTER Teacher, 1999.

Dover, Wendy. *The Personal Planner & Training Guide for the Para Professional* (3-ring binder). Manhattan, KS: MASTER Teacher, 1996.

Downing, June E. *Including Students with Severe and Multiple Disabilities in Typical Classrooms, 2nd Edition.* Baltimore, MD: Paul H. Brookes Publishing, 2001.

Doyle, Mary Beth. *The Paraprofessional's Guide to the Inclusive Classroom: Working as a Team, 2nd Edition.* Baltimore, MD: Brookes Publishing Company, 2001.

Elias, Maurice & Linda B. Butler. *Social Decision Making/Social Problem Solving A Curriculum for Academic, Social and Emotional Learning.* Champaign, IL: Research Press, 2005.

Elias, Maurice, Brian Friedlander & Steven Tobias. *Engaging the Resistant Child Through Computers: A Manual to Facilitate Social & Emotional Learning.* Port Chester, NY: Dude Publishing, 2001.

Elias, Maurice & Harriett Arnold. *The Educator's Guide to Emotional Intelligence and Academic Achievement.* Thousand Oaks, CA: Corwin Press, 2006.

Elias, Maurice & Joseph E. Zins, et al. *Promoting Social & Emotional Learning Guidelines for Educators.* Alexandria, VA: ASCD, 1997.

Elliott, Judy L. & Martha L. Thurlow. *Improving Test Performance of Students with Disabilities. On District and State Assessments.* Thousand Oaks, CA: Corwin Press, 2000.

Fad, Kathleen McConnell & James R. Patton. *Behavioral Intervention Planning.* Austin, TX: Pro-Ed, Inc., 2000.

Fisher, Douglas, Caren Sax & Ian Pumpian. *Inclusive High Schools.* Baltimore, MD: Paul H. Brookes Publishing, 1999.

Flick, Grad L. *ADD/ADHD Behavior-Change Resource Kit.* West Nyack, NY: Center for Applied Research in Education, 1998.

Friedlander, Brian S. *Assistive Technology: A Way to Differentiate Instruction for Students with Disabilities.* Port Chester, NY: National Professional Resources, Inc., 2005.

Friend, Marilyn. *Complexities of Collaboration* (Video). Bloomington, IN: Forum on Education, 2000.

Friend, Marilyn. *The Power of Two: Making a Difference Through Co-Teaching, 2nd Edition* (Video). Bloomington, IN: Forum on Education, 2004.

Friend, Marilyn. *Successful High School Inclusion: Making Access a Reality for All Students* (Video). Bloomington, IN: Forum on Education, 2001.

Friend, Marilyn & Lynne Cooke. *Interactions: Collaboration Skills for School Professionals, 4th Edition.* Boston, MA: Allyn & Bacon, 2002.

Forum on Education (Producer). *Adapting Curriculum & Instruction in Inclusive Classrooms* (Video). Bloomington, IN: 1999.

Gardner, Howard. *How Are Kids Smart?* (Video) Port Chester, NY: National Professional Resources, Inc., 1996.

Giangreco, Michael F. *Quick Guides To Inclusion 3: Ideas for Educating Students with Disabilities.* Baltimore, MD: Brookes Publishing Company, 2002.

Giangreco, Michael, Chigee J. Cloninger & Virginia Salce Iverson. *Choosing Outcomes & Accommodations for Children (COACH), 2nd Edition.* Baltimore, MD: Paul H. Brookes Publishing, 1998.

Glasser, William. *Choice Theory: A New Psychology of Personal Freedom.* New York, NY: HarperCollins, 1998.

Gold, Mimi. *Help for the Struggling Student: Ready-to-Use Strategies and Lessons to Build Attention, Memory, and Organizational Skills.* San Francisco, CA: Jossey-Bass, 2003.

Goleman, Daniel. *Emotional Intelligence: A New Vision for Educators* (Video). Port Chester, NY: National Professional Resources, Inc., 1996.

Goleman, Daniel. *Emotional Intelligence: Why It Can Matter More Than IQ.* New York, NY: Bantam Books, 1995.

Gore, M.C. *Successful Inclusion Strategies for Secondary and Middle School Teachers: Keys to Help Struggling Learners Access the Curriculum.* Thousand Oaks, CA: Corwin Press, 2003.

Gorman, Jean Cheng. *Emotional Disorders and Learning Disabilities in the Classroom: Interactions and Interventions.* Thousand Oaks, CA: Corwin Press, 2001.

Gregory, Gale & Carolyn Chapman. *Differentiated Instructional Strategies: One Size Doesn't Fit All.* Thousand Oaks, CA: Corwin Press, 2002.

Grisham-Brown, Jennifer, Mary Louise Hemmeter,& Kristie Pretti-Frontczak. *Blended Practices for Teaching Young Children in Inclusive Settings.* Baltimore, MD: Brooks Publishing, 2005.

Guilford Press (Producer). *Assessing ADHD in the Schools* (Video). New York, NY: 1999.

Guilford Press (Producer). *Classroom Interventions for ADHD* (Video). New York, NY: 1999.

Gusman, Jo. *Differentiated Instruction & the English Language Learner: Best Practices to Use With Your Students (K-12)* (Video). Port Chester, NY: National Professional Resources, Inc., 2004.

Halvorsen, Ann T. & Thomas Neary. *Building Inclusive Schools: Tools and Strategies for Success*. Boston, MA: Allyn & Bacon, 2001.

Hammeken, Peggy A. *Inclusion: 450 Strategies for Success: A Practical Guide for All Educators Who Teach Students with Disabilities, Revised Edition*. Minnetonka, MN: Peytral Publications, 2000.

Hammeken, Peggy A. *Inclusion: An Essential Guide for the Para Professional*. Minnetonka, MN: Peytral Publications, 1996.

Hannell, Glynis. *Identifying Children with Special Needs*. Thousand Oaks, CA: Corwin Press, 2005.

HBO (Producer). *Educating Peter* (Video). New York, NY: 1993.

Heacox, Diane. *Differentiated Instruction: How to Reach and Teach All Learners (Grades 3-12)*. Minneapolis, MN: Free Spirit Press, 2002.

Hehir, Thomas. *New Directions in Special Education*. Cambridge, MA: Harvard University Press, 2005.

Iervolino, Constance & Helene Hanson. *Differentiated Instructional Practice Video Series: A Focus on Inclusion (Tape 1), A Focus on the Gifted (Tape 2)*. Port Chester, NY: National Professional Resources, Inc. 2003.

Janney, Rachel & Martha E. Snell. *Behavioral Support: Teachers' Guides to Inclusive Practices*. Baltimore, MD: Paul H. Brookes Publishing Co., Inc., 2000.

Janney, Rachel & Martha E. Snell. *Collaborative Teaming: Teachers' Guides to Inclusive Practices*. Baltimore, MD: Brookes Publishing Company, 2000.

Janney, Rachel & Martha E. Snell. *Modifying Schoolwork: Teachers' Guides to Inclusive Practices, 2nd Edition*. Baltimore, MD: Paul H. Brookes Publishing Co., Inc., 2004.

Jensen, Eric. *Different Brains, Different Learners: How to Reach the Hard to Reach*. San Diego, CA: The Brain Store, 2000.

Jensen, Eric. *The Fragile Brain: What Impairs Learning and What We Can Do About It*. Port Chester, NY: National Professional Resources, Inc., 2000.

Jensen, Eric. *Practical Applications of Brain-Based Learning*. Port Chester, NY: National Professional Resources, Inc., 2000.

Jorgensen, Cheryl M. *Restructuring High Schools for All Students.* Baltimore, MD: Paul H. Brookes Publishing, 1998.

Jorgensen Cheryl M., Mary C. Schuh, & Jan Nisbet. *The Inclusion Facilitator's Guide.* Baltimore, MD: Brooks Publishing, 2006.

Kagan, Spencer & Laurie Kagan. *Reaching Standards Through Cooperative Learning: Providing for ALL Learners in General Education Classrooms* (4-video series). Port Chester, NY: National Professional Resources, Inc., 1999.

Kagan, Spencer & Miguel Kagan. *Multiple Intelligences: The Complete MI Book.* San Clemente, CA: Kagan Cooperative Learning, 1998.

Kame'enui, Edward J. & Deborah C. Simmons. *Adapting Curricular Materials, Volume 1: An Overview of Materials Adaptations – Toward Successful Inclusion of Students with Disabilities: The Architecture of Instruction.* Reston, VA: Council for Exceptional Children, 1999.

Karten, Toby J. *Inclusion Strategies That Work!: Research-Based Methods for the Classroom.* Thousand Oaks, CA: Corwin Press, 2004.

Katzman, Lauren I. & Allison G. Gandhi (Editors). *Special Education for a New Century.* Cambridge, MA: Harvard Educational Review, 2005.

Kennedy, Craig H. & Douglas Fisher. *Inclusive Middle Schools.* Baltimore, MD: Paul H. Brookes Publishing, 2001.

Kennedy, Eugene. *Raising Test Scores for All Students: An Administrator's Guide to Improving Standardized Test Performance.* Thousand Oaks, CA: Corwin Press, 2003.

Kleinert, Harold L. & Jacqui F. Kearns. *Alternate assessment: Measuring Outcomes and Supports for Students with Disabilities.* Baltimore, MD: Brookes Publishing Company, Inc., 2001.

Kliewer, Christopher. *Schooling Children with Down Syndrome.* New York, NY: Teachers College Press, 1998.

Kluth, Paula, Diana M. Straut & Douglas P. Biklen. *Access to Academics for All Students: Critical   Approaches to Inclusive Curriculum, Instruction, and Policy.* Mahwah, NJ: Lawrence Erlbaum Associates, Inc., 2003.

Koegel, Lynn Kern, Robert Koegel & Glen Dunlap (Editors). *Positive Behavioral Support: Including People with Difficult Behavior in the Community.* Baltimore, MD: Brookes Publishing Company, Inc., 1996.

Kugelmass, Judy W. *The Inclusive School: Sustaining Equity and Standards.* New York, NY: Teachers College Press, 2004.

Lavoie, Richard. *Beyond F.A.T. City* (Video). Charlotte, NC: PBS Video, 2005.

Lavoie, Richard. *F.A.T. City: How Difficult Can This Be?* (Video). Charlotte, NC: PBS Video, 1989.

Lavoie, Richard. *It's So Much Work to Be Your Friend* (Video). Charlotte, NC: PBS Video, 2005.

Levine, Mel. *A Mind at a Time.* New York, NY: Simon & Schuster, 2002.

Lickona, Thomas. *Character Matters.* New York, NY: Touchstone, 2004.

Lickona, Thomas. *Educating for Character: How Our Schools Can Teach Respect and Responsibility.* New York, NY: Bantam, 1992.

Lipsky, Dorothy K. & Alan Gartner. *Inclusion: A Service, Not A Place – A Whole School Approach* (Video). Port Chester, NY: National Professional Resources, Inc., 2002.

Lipsky, Dorothy K. & Alan Gartner. *Inclusion and School Reform: Transforming America's Classrooms.* Baltimore, MD: Paul H. Brookes Publishing, 1997.

Lipsky, Dorothy K. & Alan Gartner. *Standards & Inclusion: Can We Have Both?* (Video). Port Chester, NY: National Professional Resources, Inc., 1998.

Long, Nicholas, & William Morse. *Conflict in the Classroom: The Education of At-Risk and Troubled Students, 5th Edition.* Austin, TX: Pro-Ed, Inc., 1996.

Maanum, Jody L. *The General Educator's Guide to Special Education, 2nd Edition.* Minnetonka, MN: Peytral Publications, Inc., 2003.

MASTER Teacher (Producer). *Lesson Plans & Modifications for Inclusion and Collaborative Classrooms* (4-video series). Manhattan, KS: 1995.

Maurer, Marvin & Marc Brackett. *Emotional Literacy in the Middle School.* Port Chester, NY: Dude Publishing, 2004.

McCarney, Stephen B. *The Pre-Referral Intervention Manual.* Columbia, MO: Hawthorne Educational Services, 1993.

McGregor, Gail & R. Timm Vogelsberg. *Inclusive Schooling Practices: Pedagogical and Research Foundations.* Baltimore, MD: Paul H. Brooks Publishing Co., Inc. 1998.

McNary, Sarah J., Neal A. Glasgow & Cathy D. Hicks. *What Successful Teachers Do in Inclusive Classrooms: 60 Research-Based Teaching Strategies That Special Learners Succeed.* Thousand Oaks, CA: Corwin Press, 2005.

McPartland, Pat. *Implementing Ongoing Transition Plans for the IEP: A Student-Driven Approach to IDEA Mandates.* Verona, WI: Attainment Company, Inc., 2005.

Minskoff, Esther & David Allsopp. *Academic Success Strategies for Adolescents with Learning Disabilities & ADHD.* Baltimore, MD: Paul H. Brookes Publishing, 2002.

Moll, Anne M. *Differentiated Instruction Guide for Inclusive Teaching.* Port Chester, NY: Dude Publishing, 2003.

Munk, Dennis D. *Solving the Grading Puzzle for Students with Disabilities.* Whitefish Bay, WI: Knowledge by Design, Inc., 2003.

National Association of State Directors of Special Education (NASDSE). *Response to Intervention: Policy, Considerations, and Implementation.* Alexandria, VA: NASDSE, 2005.

Nelsen, Jane, Lynn Lott & H. Stephen Glenn. *Positive Discipline In The Classroom: Developing Mutual Respect, Cooperation, and Responsibility in Your Classroom.* Three Rivers, MI: Three Rivers Press, 2000.

Nolet, Victor & Margaret McLaughlin. *Accessing the General Curriculum: Including Students with Disabilities in Standards-Based Reform.* Thousand Oaks, CA: Corwin Press, 2000.

Norlander, Karen. *RTI Tackles the LD Explosion: A Good IDEA Becomes Law (Video).* Port Chester, NY: National Professional Resources, Inc., 2006.

Nunley, Kathie F. *Differentiating the High School Classroom.* Thousand Oaks, CA: Corwin Publishing, 2005.

Nunley, Kathie F. *Layered Curriculum.* Amherst, NH: Brains.org, 2004.

Pierangelo, Roger. *Special Educator's Book of Lists, 2nd Edition.* West Nyack, NY: Center for Applied Research in Education, 2003.

Porter, Stephanie, et al. *Children and Youth – Assisted by Medical Technology in Educational Settings: Guidelines for Care.* Baltimore, MD: Paul H. Brookes Publishing, 1997.

Purcell, Sherry & Debbie Grant. *Using Assistive Technology to Meet Literacy Standards.* Verona, WI: IEP Resources, 2004.

Putnam, Joanne W. *Cooperative Learning and Strategies for Inclusion.* Baltimore, MD: Paul H. Brookes Publishing, 1998.

Reider, Barbara. *Teach More and Discipline Less.* Thousand Oaks, CA: Corwin Press, 2005.

Renzulli, Joseph S. *Developing the Gifts and Talents of ALL Students: The Schoolwide Enrichment Model* (Video). Port Chester, NY: National Professional Resources, Inc., 1999.

Rief, Sandra F. *The ADD/ADHD Checklist.* Paramus, NJ: Prentice Hall, 1998.

Rief, Sandra F. *ADHD & LD: Powerful Teaching Strategies & Accommodations* (Video). Port Chester, NY: National Professional Resources, Inc., 2004.

Rief, Sandra F. *How to Help Your Child Succeed in School: Strategies and Guidance for Parents of Children with ADHD and/or Learning Disabilities* (Video). Port Chester, NY: National Professional Resources, Inc., 1997.

Rief, Sandra F. & Julie A. Heimburge. *How to Reach & Teach All Students in the Inclusive Classroom: Ready-To-Use Strategies, Lessons, and Activities for Teaching Students with Learning Needs.* West Nyack, NY: Center for Applied Research in Education, 1996.

Robinson, Viviane & Mei K. Lai. *Practitioner Research for Educators.* Thousand Oaks, CA: Corwin Press, 2006.

Rose, D. & A. Meyer (Editors). *Teaching Every Student in the Digital Age.* Alexandria, VA: ASCD, 2002.

Rose, D. & A. Meyer (Editors). *The Universally Designed Classroom: Accessible Curriculum and Digital Technologies.* Cambridge, MA: Harvard University Press, 2005.

Rutherford, Paula. *Instruction for All Students.* Alexandria, VA: Just Ask Publications, 2002.

Ryan, Kevin & Karen E. Bohlin. *Building Character in Schools: Practical Ways to Bring Moral Instruction to Life.* San Francisco, CA: Jossey-Bass, 2003.

Sailor, Wayne. *Creating A Unified System: Integrating General and Special Education for the Benefit of All Students* (Video). Bloomington, IN: Forum on Education, 2004.

Sailor, Wayne. *Whole-School Success and Inclusive Education: Building Partnerships for Learning, Achievement, and Accountability.* New York, NY: Teachers College Press, 2002.

Salovey, Peter. *Optimizing Intelligences: Thinking, Emotion, and Creativity* (Video). Port Chester, NY: National Professional Resources, Inc., 1998.

Sapon-Shevin, Mara. *Because We Can Change the World: A Practical Guide to Building Cooperative, Inclusive Classroom Communities.* Boston, MA: Allyn & Bacon, 1999.

Schumaker, Jean & Keith Lenz. *Adapting Curricular Materials, Volume 3: Grades Six Through Eight – Adapting Language Arts, Social Studies, and Science Materials for the Inclusive Classroom.* Reston, VA: Council for Exceptional Children, 1999.

Schwarz, Shelley Peterman & Nancy Kruschke McKinney. *Organizing your IEPs.* Verona, WI: Attainment Company, Inc., 2005.

Scully, Jennifer L. *The Power of Social Skills in Character Development: Helping Diverse Learners Succeed.* Port Chester, NY: Dude Publishing, 2000.

Shaywitz, Sally. *Overcoming Dyslexia: A New and Complete Science-Based Program for Reading Problems at Any Level.* New York, NY: Knopf Publishing, 2003.

Shore, Kenneth. *The ABCs of Bullying Prevention.* Port Chester, NY: Dude Publishing, 2005.

Shumm, Jeanne Shay. *Adapting Curricular Materials, Volume 2: Kindergarten Through Grade Five – Adapting Reading & Math Materials for the Inclusive Classroom.* Reston, VA: Council for Exceptional Children, 1999.

Siegel, Lawrence M. *Complete IEP Guide: How to Advocate for Your Special Ed Child, 2nd Edition.* Berkeley, CA: NOLO, 2001.

Smith, Sally. *Teach Me Different!* (Video). Charlotte, NC: PBS Video, 2001.

Snell, Martha E. & Rachel Janney. *Collaborative Teaming.* Baltimore, MD: Paul H. Brookes Publishing Co., Inc., 2000.

Snell, Martha E. & Rachel Janney. *Social Relationships & Peer Support.* Baltimore, MD: Paul H. Brookes Publishing Co., Inc., 2000.

Snell, Martha E. & Rachel Janney. *Teachers' Guides to Inclusive Practices.* Baltimore, MD: Brookes Publishing Company, Inc., 2000.

Sousa, David A. *How the Special Needs Brain Learns.* Thousand Oaks, CA: Corwin Press, 2001.

Stainback, Susan & William Stainback. *Inclusion: A Guide for Educators.* Baltimore, MD: Paul H. Brookes Publishing, 1996.

Stirling, Diane, G. Archibald, L. McKay & S. Berg. *Character Education Connections for School, Home and Community: A Guide for Integrating Character Education.* Port Chester, NY: National Professional Resources, Inc., 2001.

Strichart, Stephen S., Charles T. Mangrum II & Patricia Iannuzzi. *Teaching Study Skills* and Strategies to Students with Learning Disabilities, Attention Deficit Disorders, *or Special Needs, 2nd Edition.* Boston, MA: Allyn & Bacon, 1998.

Stride, June. Practical Strategies in Elementary School Inclusion. Verona, WI: Attainment Company, Inc., 2005.

Teele, Sue. *Rainbows of Intelligence: Raising Student Performance Through Multiple Intelligences* (Video). Port Chester, NY: National Professional Resources, Inc., 2000.

Thompson, Sandra, Rachel Quenemeen, Martha Thurlow, & James Ysseldyke. *Alternate Assessments for Students with Disabilities.* Thousand Oaks, CA: Corwin Press, 2001.

Thorne, Beverly. *Hands-On Activities for Exceptional Students: Education and Pre-Vocational Activities for Students with Cognitive Delays.* Minnetonka, MN: Peytral Publications, 2001.

Thousand, Jacqueline S., Richard A. Villa & Ann I. Nevin. *Creativity and Collaborative Learning: The Practical Guide to Empowering Students, Teachers, and Families, 2ⁿᵈ Edition.* Baltimore, MD: Paul H. Brookes Publishing, 2002.

Thurlow, Martha L., Judy L. Elliott & James E. Ysseldyke. *Testing Students with Disabilities: Practical   Strategies for Complying With District and State Requirements.* Thousand Oaks, CA: Corwin   Press, 1998.

Tilton, Linda. *Teacher's Toolbox for Differentiating Instruction: 700 Strategies, Tips, Tools, & Techniques.* Shorewood, MN: Covington Cove Publications, 2003.

Tomlinson, Carol Ann. *How to Differentiate Instruction in Mixed-Ability Classrooms, 2nd Edition.* Alexandria, VA: ASCD, 2001.

Twachtman-Cullen, Diane & Jennifer Twachtman-Reilly. *How Well Does Your IEP Measure Up?: Quality Indicators for Effective Service Delivery.* Higganum, CT: Starfish Specialty Press, 2002.

Van Dover, Teresa. *The Inclusion Guide for Handling Chronically Disruptive Behavior.* Manhattan, KS: MASTER Teacher, 1996.

Villa, Richard A. *Collaboration for Inclusion Video Series* (Video Set). Port Chester, NY: National Professional Resources, Inc. 2002.

Villa, Richard A. & Jacqueline S. Thousand. *A Guide to Co-Teaching.* Thousand Oaks, CA: Corwin Press, 2004.

Villa, Richard A. & Jacqueline S. Thousand. *Creating An Inclusive School, 2nd Edition.* Alexandria, VA: Association for Supervision & Curriculum Development, 2005.

Villa, Richard A. & Jacqueline S. Thousand. *Restructuring for Caring and Effective Education: Piecing the Puzzle Together, 2nd Edition.* Baltimore, MD: Paul H. Brookes Publishing, 2000.

Wagner, Sheila. *Inclusive Programming For Elementary Students With Autism.* Arlington, TX: Future Horizons, 1999.

Watson, T. Steuart & Mark W. Steege. *Conducting School-Based Functional Behavioral Assessments: A Practitioner's Guide.* New York, NY: Guilford Press, 2003.

Wood, M. Mary & Nicholas Long. *Life Space Intervention: Talking with Children and Youth in Crisis.* Austin, TX: Pro-Ed, Inc., 1991.

Wormel, Rick. *Fair Isn't Always Equal.* Portland, ME: Stenhouse Publishers, 2006.

Wright, Pam & Pete Wright. *Wrightslaw: From Emotions to Advocacy – The Special Education Survival Guide.* Hartfield, VA: Harbor House Law Press, Inc., 2001.

Wright, Peter W. D. & Pamela Darr Wright. *Wrightslaw: Special Education Law.* Hartfield, VA: Harbor House Law Press, Inc., 1999.

Wright, Peter W. D., Pamela Darr Wright & Suzanne Whitney Heath. *Wrightslaw: No Child Left Behind.* Hartfield, VA: Harbor House Law Press, Inc., 2003.

Wunderlich, Kathy C. *The Teacher's Guide to Behavioral Interventions.* Columbia, MO: Hawthorne Educational Services, Inc., 1988.

About the Author

Dr. Lisa Dieker is an Associate Professor and the Lockheed Martin Eminent Scholar Chair in the College of Education at the University of Central Florida (UCF). At UCF she coordinates the doctoral program in special education and is the Director of the Lockheed Martin Mathematics and Science Academy. Dr. Dieker is committed to examining ways to utilize technology, specifically streamed-video and virtual classrooms, to impact teacher preparation. Her primary area of research focuses on collaboration between general and special educators at the secondary level, with a specific interest in the unique opportunities that exist in urban schools.

Having received her undergraduate and master's degree from Eastern Illinois University and her Ph.D. from the University of Illinois, Dr. Dieker served for nine years on the faculty at the University of Wisconsin-Milwaukee where she chaired the secondary program and co-directed a project that certified over 150 teachers to work in urban schools. She is the author of *The Co-Teaching Lesson Plan Book* and is the featured presenter on the video/DVD production, *7 Effective Strategies for Secondary Inclusion*. She has published numerous articles on reflective thinking, teacher assistance teams, co-teaching and secondary inclusion. She currently serves on numerous editorial review boards and is the co-editor of the *Journal of International Special Needs Education* and an Associate Editor for the *Journal of Psychological and Educational Consulting*.